St.George's, Grenada

Dave Knight

Contents

Articles

Overview of Grenada

Grenada

Grenada

Motto: "Ever Conscious of God We Aspire, Build and Advance as One People"

Anthem: *Hail Grenada*
Royal anthem: *God Save the Queen*

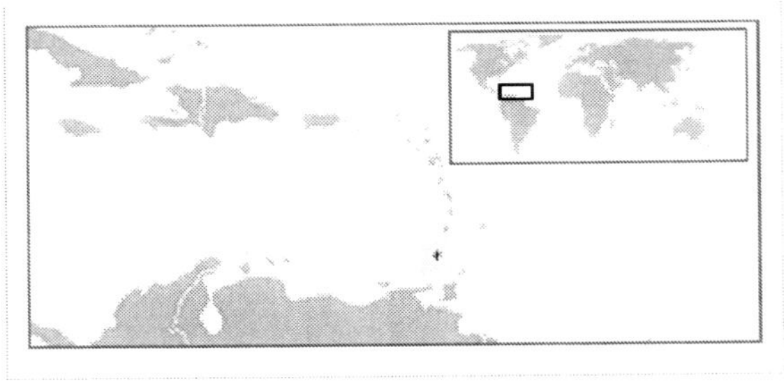

Capital (and largest city)	St. George's 12°03′N 61°45′W
Official language(s)	English
Ethnic groups	82% black, 13% mixed black and European, 5% European and East Indian, and trace of Arawak/Carib
Demonym	Grenadian, Greenz, Greens
Government	Parliamentary democracy under constitutional monarchy
- Queen	Queen Elizabeth II
- Governor General	Carlyle Glean
- Prime Minister	Tillman Thomas
Legislature	Parliament

-	Upper House	Senate
-	Lower House	House of Representatives
Independence from the United Kingdom		
-	Date	Thursday 7 February 1974
Area		
-	Total	344 km^2 (203rd) 132.8 sq mi
-	Water (%)	1.6
Population		
-	July 12, 2005 estimate	110,000 (185th)
-	Density	319.8/km^2 (45th) 828.3/sq mi
GDP (PPP)		2009 estimate
-	Total	$1.103 billion
-	Per capita	$10,712
GDP (nominal)		2009 estimate
-	Total	$615 million
-	Per capita	$5,969
HDI (2007)		▲ 0.813 (high) (74th)
Currency		East Caribbean dollar (XCD)
Time zone		(UTC−4)
-	Summer (DST)	(UTC−4)
Drives on the		left
ISO 3166 code		GD
Internet TLD		.gd
Calling code		+1-473
[a] 2002 estimate.		

Grenada (pronounced /ɡrɨˈneɪdə/ (listen)) is an island country and Commonwealth Realm consisting of the island of Grenada and six smaller islands at the southern end of the Grenadines in the southeastern Caribbean Sea. Grenada is located northwest of Trinidad and Tobago, northeast of

Venezuela, and southwest of Saint Vincent and the Grenadines.

Grenada is also known as the "Island of Spice" due to the production of nutmeg and mace crops of which Grenada is one of the world's largest exporters.

Its size is 344 square kilometres (133 sq mi), with an estimated population of 110,000. Its capital is St. George's. The national bird of Grenada is the critically endangered Grenada Dove.

History

Main article: History of Grenada

1498–1958: Colonization

The recorded history of Grenada begins in 1498. At the time the indigenous Island Caribs (Kalinago) who lived there called it Camahogne. The Spaniards did not permanently settle on Camahogne. Later the English failed their first settlement attempts, but the French fought and conquered Grenada from the Caribs circa 1650. The French conquest resulted in the genocide of 17th century Caribs from present-day Grenada. Warfare also existed between the Caribs of present day Dominica and St. Vincent and the Grenadines with the French invaders.

The French took control of Camahogne and named the new French colony La Grenade. La Grenade prospered as a wealthy French colony; its main export was sugar. The French established a capital known as Fort Royal in 1650 as ordered by Cardinal Richelieu. To wait out harsh hurricanes, the French navy would shelter in the capital's natural harbour. No other French colony had a natural harbour to even compare with that of Fort Royal (later renamed St. George's). The French captured the island but formally ceded it to Great Britain in 1783 by the Treaty of Paris. A century later, in 1877 Grenada was made a Crown Colony. [citation needed]

1958–1983: Independence and Revolution

The capital St. George's, Grenada

The island was a province of the short-lived West Indies Federation from 1958 to 1962.

In 1967, Grenada attained the status of "Associated State of the United Kingdom", which meant that Grenada was now responsible for her own internal affairs, and the UK was responsible for her defence and foreign affairs. Independence was granted in 1974 under the leadership of the then Premier, Sir Eric Matthew Gairy, who became the first Prime Minister of Grenada.

Civil conflict gradually broke out between Eric Gairy's government and some opposition parties including the New Jewel Movement (NJM). Gairy's party won elections in 1976 but the opposition did not accept the result, accusing it of fraudulence. In 1979, the New Jewel Movement under Maurice Bishop launched a paramilitary attack on the government resulting in its overthrow.

The constitution was suspended and Bishop's government ruled subsequently by decree. Cuban presence was welcomed and heavily invested in civic assistance (doctors, teachers, and technicians in the fields of health, literacy, agriculture, and agro-industries) during the ensuing era. Agrarian reforms started by the Gairy government were continued and greatly expanded under the revolutionary government of Maurice Bishop.

1983: Invasion of Grenada by the U.S. and OECS military

Main article: Invasion of Grenada

Members of the Eastern Caribbean Defence Force during the Invasion of Grenada.

Some years later a dispute developed between Bishop and certain high-ranking members of the NJM. Though Bishop was cooperating with Cuba and the USSR on various trade and foreign policy issues, he sought to maintain a "non-aligned" status. Bishop had been taking his time making Grenada wholly socialist, encouraging private-sector development in an attempt to make the island a popular tourist destination. Hardline Marxist party members, including Communist Deputy Prime Minister Bernard Coard, deemed Bishop insufficiently revolutionary and demanded that he either step down or enter into a power sharing arrangement.[citation needed]

On October 19, 1983, Bernard Coard and his wife Phyllis, backed by the Grenadian Army, led a coup against the government of Maurice Bishop, who was placed under house arrest. These actions led to street demonstrations in various parts of the island. Bishop had massive support among the population and was eventually freed by a large demonstration in the capital. When Bishop attempted to resume power, he was captured and executed by soldiers along with seven others, including government cabinet ministers. The Coard regime then put the island under martial law.[citation needed]

After the execution of Bishop, the People's Revolutionary Army formed a military government with General Hudson Austin as chairman. The army declared a four-day total curfew during which it said that anyone leaving their home without approval would be shot on sight.

The overthrow of a moderate government by one which was strongly pro-communist worried U.S. President Ronald Reagan. Of particular concern was the presence of Cuban construction workers and military personnel building a 10000-foot (3000 m) airstrip on Grenada. Though Bishop had claimed the purpose of the airstrip was to allow commercial jets to land, U.S. military analysts believed the only reason for constructing an abnormally long, reinforced runway was for the use of heavy military transport planes. Reagan was worried that Grenada would be used by Cuba under the direction of the Soviet Union as a refueling stepping stone for Cuban and Soviet airplanes loaded with weapons destined for Central American communist insurgents.

On October 25, Grenada was invaded by combined forces from the United States, the Regional Security System (RSS) and Jamaica, in an operation codenamed *Operation Urgent Fury*. The U.S. stated this was done at the behest of Dame Eugenia Charles, of Dominica. While the Governor-General, Sir Paul Scoon, later stated that he had also requested the invasion, it was highly criticised by HM Queen Elizabeth II and the governments of the United Kingdom, Trinidad and Tobago and Canada. The United Nations General Assembly condemned it as "a flagrant violation of international law" by a vote of 108 in favor to 9, with 27 abstentions. The United Nations Security Council considered a similar resolution, which failed to pass when vetoed by the United States.[*citation needed*]

After the invasion of the island nation, the pre-revolutionary Grenadan constitution was resumed. Eighteen members of the PRG and the PRA (army) were arrested after the invasion on charges related to the murder of Maurice Bishop and seven others. The eighteen included the top political leadership of Grenada at the time of the execution as well as the entire military chain of command directly responsible for the operation that led to the executions. Fourteen were sentenced to death, one was found not guilty and three were sentenced to forty-five years in prison. The death sentences were eventually commuted to terms of imprisonment. Those in prison have become known as the Grenada 17.

Since 1983

In 2000–2002, much of the controversy of the late 1970s and early 1980s was once again brought into the public consciousness with the opening of the truth and reconciliation commission. The commission was chaired by a Roman Catholic priest, Father Mark Haynes, and was tasked with uncovering injustices arising from the PRA, Bishop's regime, and before. It held a number of hearings around the country. Brother Robert Fanovich, head of Presentation Brothers' College (PBC) in St. George's tasked some of his senior students with conducting a research project into the era and specifically into the fact that Maurice Bishop's body was never discovered. See Maurice Paterson's book, published before this event, called *Big Sky Little Bullet*. Paterson also uncovered that there was still a lot of resentment in Grenadian society resulting from the era, and a feeling that there were many injustices still unaddressed.

In 2004, after being hurricane-free for forty-nine years, the island was directly hit by Hurricane Ivan (September 7). Ivan struck as a Category 3 hurricane and caused 90 percent of the homes to be damaged or destroyed. The following year, 2005, Hurricane Emily (July 14), a Category 1 hurricane at the time, struck the northern part of the island with 80 knots (150 km/h; 92 mph) winds, causing an estimated USD $110 million (EC$ 297 million) worth of damage. This was much less damage than Ivan had caused.[citation needed]

Grenada has recovered with remarkable speed, due to both domestic labour and financing from the world at large and the work done by the New National Party Administration of Dr. Keith Mitchell and his team. By December 2005, 96% of all hotel rooms were to be open for business and to have been upgraded in facilities and strengthened to an improved building code. The agricultural industry and in particular the nutmeg industry suffered serious losses, but that event has begun changes in crop management and it is hoped that as new nutmeg trees gradually mature, the industry will return to its pre-Ivan position as a major supplier in the Western world.[citation needed]

In April 2007, Grenada jointly hosted (along with several other Caribbean nations) the 2007 Cricket World Cup. The island's then Prime Minister was at the time CARICOM Representative on cricket and was instrumental in having the World Cup Games brought to the region. After Hurricane Ivan, the government of the People's Republic of China (PRC) paid for the new $40 million national stadium, and provided the aid of over 300 labourers to build and repair it. During the opening ceremony, the anthem of the Republic of China (ROC, Taiwan) was accidentally played instead of the PRC's anthem, leading to the firing of top officials.

Geography

Main article: Geography of Grenada

The island Grenada itself is the largest island; smaller Grenadines are Carriacou, Petit Martinique, Ronde Island, Caille Island, Diamond Island, Large Island, Saline Island, and Frigate Island. Most of the population lives on Grenada itself, and major towns there include the capital, St. George's, Grenville and Gouyave. The largest settlement on the other islands is Hillsborough on Carriacou.

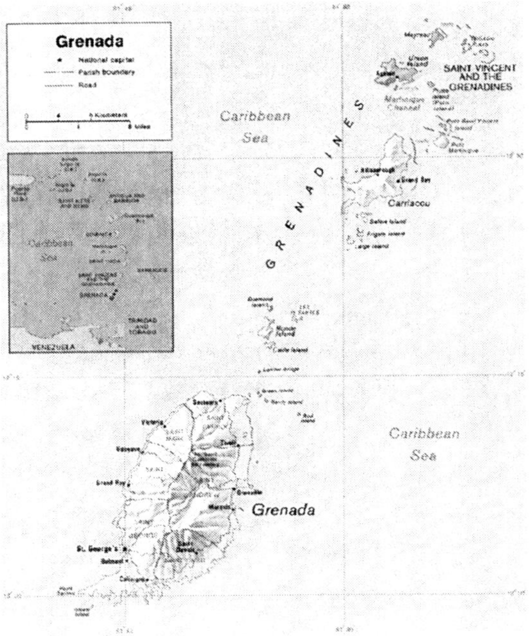

The islands are of volcanic origin with extremely rich soil. Grenada's interior is very mountainous with Mount St. Catherine being the highest at 2756 feet (840 m). Several small rivers with beautiful waterfalls flow into the sea from these mountains. The climate is tropical: hot and humid in the rainy season and cooled by the trade winds in the dry season. Grenada, being on the Southern edge of the hurricane belt, has suffered only three hurricanes in fifty years.

A view of Carriacou. Other Grenadine islands in distance

Hurricane Janet passed over Grenada on Friday 23 September 1955 with winds of 115 mph (185 km/h), causing severe damage. The most recent storms to hit have been Hurricane Ivan on Tuesday 7 September 2004 causing severe damage and thirty-nine deaths and Hurricane Emily on Thursday 14 July 2005, causing serious damage in Carriacou and in the north of Grenada which had been relatively lightly affected by Hurricane Ivan.

National Icon

National	Icon
Dish	Oil Down
Symbol	Nutmeg
Drink	Rum
Sport	Cricket Soccer
Bird	Grenada Dove
Song	Grenada May God Bless You
National Pledge	Pledge of Allegiance

Parishes

Main article: Parishes of Grenada

Grenada is divided into 6 parishes:

1. Saint Andrew
2. Saint David
3. Saint George
4. Saint John
5. Saint Mark
6. Saint Patrick

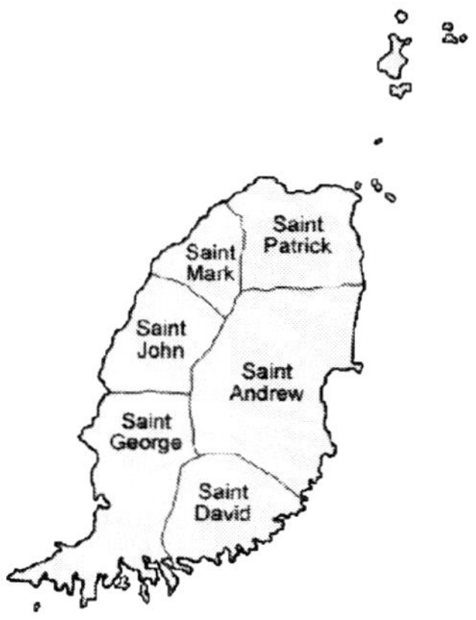

Parishes of Grenada

Carriacou and Petite Martinique, two of the Grenadines, have the status of dependency.

Politics

Main article: Politics of Grenada

As a Commonwealth realm, Queen Elizabeth II is Queen of Grenada and Head of State. The Crown is represented by a Governor-General, who is currently Mr. Carlyle Glean. Day-to-day executive power lies with the Head of Government, the Prime Minister. Although appointed by the Governor-General, the Prime Minister is usually the leader of the largest party in the Parliament.

The Parliament consists of a Senate (thirteen members) and a House of Representatives (fifteen members). The senators are appointed by the government and the opposition, while the representatives are elected by the population for five-year terms. With 51% of the votes and eleven seats in the 2008 election, the National Democratic Congress won the July 8, 2008 election. The opposition New National Party won the remaining four seats.

Grenada is a full and participating member of both the Caribbean Community (CARICOM) and the Organisation of Eastern Caribbean States (OECS).

Economy and tourism

Main article: Economy of Grenada

Economic progress in fiscal reforms and prudent macroeconomic management have boosted annual growth to 5%–6% in 1998–99; the increase in economic activity has been led by construction and trade. Tourist facilities are being expanded; tourism is the leading foreign exchange earner. Major short-term concerns are the rising fiscal deficit and the deterioration in the external account balance. Grenada shares a common central bank and a common currency (the East Caribbean dollar) with seven other members of the Organisation of Eastern Caribbean States (OECS)

Grenada is called **The Spice Isle** because it is a leading producer of several different spices. Cinnamon, cloves, ginger, mace, allspice, orange/citrus peels, wild coffee used by the locals, and especially nutmeg, providing 20% of the world supply, are all important exports. The nutmeg on the nation's flag represents the economic crop of Grenada; the nation is the world's second largest producer of nutmeg (after Indonesia).

Devastation caused by Hurricane Ivan in Grenada.

Tourism is Grenada's main economic force. Conventional beach and water-sports tourism is largely focused in the southwest region around St Georges, the airport and the coastal strip; however, ecotourism is growing in significance. Most of these small ecofriendly guesthouses are located in the Saint David and Saint John parishes. You will find a lot of different accommodations from luxury like the Spice Island Beach Resort [1] to small cottages resorts like Mango Bay Cottages [2].The tourism industry is increasing dramatically with the construction of a large cruise ship pier and esplanade. Up to 4 cruise ships per day were visiting St. Georges in 2007–8 during the cruise ship season.

The island has also pioneered the cultivation of organic cocoa which is also processed into finished bars by the Grenada Chocolate Company.

Tourism is concentrated in the southwest of the island, around St. Georges, Grand Anse, Lance Aux Epines, and Point Salines. Grenada has many idyllic beaches around its coastline including the 3 km (1.9 mi) long Grand Anse Beach in St George's which is considered to be one of the finest beaches in the world, and often appears in countdowns of the world's top 10 beaches.

Grenada is linked to the world through the Maurice Bishop International Airport and the St. George's harbour. International flights connect with other Caribbean islands, the United States, and Europe. There is also a daily fast ferry service between St. George's and Hillsborough. Beginning in October,

2009, new passenger ferry service between Grenada, Barbados, St. Vincent, St. Lucia, and Trinidad provided by Grenada-based BEDY Ocean Line is scheduled to begin.

Demographics

Main article: Demographics of Grenada

A majority of the citizens are descendants of the African slaves brought by the English and French; few of the indigenous Carib and Arawak population survived the French purge at Sauteurs. A small percentage of descendants of East Indian indentured workers were brought to Grenada mainly from the North Indian states of Bihar and Uttar Pradesh between Friday 1 May 1857–Saturday 10 January 1885. There is also a small community of French and English descendants. The rest of the population is of mixed descent.

A school on Grand Anse beach

Grenada, like many of the Caribbean islands is subject to a large amount of migration, with a large number of young people wanting to leave the island to seek life elsewhere. With just 110,000 people living in Grenada, estimates and census data suggest that there are at least that number of Grenadian-born people in other parts of the Caribbean (such as Barbados and Trinidad) and at least that number again in First World countries. Popular migration points for Grenadians further north include New York City, Toronto, the United Kingdom (London and Yorkshire predominantly — see Grenadians in the UK) and sometimes Montreal, or as far south as Australia. This means that probably around a third of those born in Grenada still live there.

The official language, English, is used in the government, but Grenadian Creole is considered the lingua franca of the island. French Patois (Antillean Creole) is also spoken by about 10%–20% the population. Some Hindi/Bhojpuri terms are still spoken amongst the Indian descendants, mostly those pertaining to the kitchen; such as *aloo, geera, karela, seim, chownkay, and baylay.* The term *bhai,* which means 'brother' or 'partner' in Hindi, is a common form of greeting amongst Indo-Grenadians males of equal status.

Religion

Religion in Grenada

religion	percent
Christianity	99.8%
Roman Catholicism	53%
Anglicanism	13.8%
Other Protestantism	33%
Rastafarian/Spiritist	1.3%
Hinduism	0.7%
Islam	0.3%
Buddhism	0.2%
Baha'is	0.2%

Grenada is a very religious country. Aside from a marginal community of Rastafarians living in Grenada, nearly all of the population belong to Christian churches. About half of the population are Roman Catholics; Anglicanism is the largest Protestant denomination with Presbyterian and Seventh Day Adventist taking up the remainder. Most churches have denomination-based schools but are open to all. There is a small Muslim population descended mostly from Gujarati Indian immigrants who came during the colonial period and set up merchant shops.

Culture

Main articles: Culture of Grenada and Music of Grenada

See also: Cricket in the West Indies

Although French influence on Grenadian culture is much less visible than on other Caribbean islands, surnames and place names in French remain, and the every day language is laced with French words and the local dialect or Patois. Stronger French influence is found in the well seasoned spicy food and styles of cooking similar to those found in New Orleans and some French architecture has survived from the 1700s. Island culture is heavily influenced by the African roots of most of the Grenadians but Indian and Carib Amerindian influence is also seen with dhal puri, rotis, Indian sweets, cassava and curries in the cuisine.

1965 carnival

The "oildown" is considered to be the national dish. The phrase "oil-down" refers to a dish cooked in coconut milk until all the milk is absorbed, leaving a bit of coconut oil in the bottom of the pot. Early recipes call for a mixture of salted pigtail, pigs feet (trotters), salt beef and chicken, dumplings made from flour, provision: breadfruit, green banana, yam and potatoes. Callaloo leaves are some times used to retain the steam and for extra flavour.

This dish is a common tradition at family and other gatherings at the beach, There is a modest debate in the West Indies about the origin of this dish, with some experts attributing it to other islands like Barbados or Trinidad & Tobago. [*citation needed*]

Foods aren't the only important aspect of Grenadian culture. Music, dance, and festivals are also extremely important. Soca, calypso, and reggae set the mood for Grenada's annual Carnival activities. Over the years Rap music became famous among Grenadian youths and there have been numerous young rappers emerging in the islands underground rap scene. Zouk is also being slowly introduced onto the island. The islanders' African and Carib Amerindian heritage plays an influential role in many aspects of Grenada's culture.

As with other islands from the Caribbean, cricket is the national and most popular sport and is an intrinsic part of Grenadian culture.

An important aspect of Grenadian culture is the tradition of story telling, with folk tales bearing both African and French influences. The character, *Anancy*, a spider god who is a trickster, originated in West Africa and is prevalent on other Caribbean islands as well. French influence can be seen in *La Diablesse*, a well-dressed she-devil, and *Ligaroo* (from Loup Garoux), a werewolf.

See also

Main article: Outline of Grenada

- Index of Grenada-related articles
- List of international rankings
- Outline of geography
- Outline of North America

Member of

- Commonwealth of Nations
- United Nations

Bibliography

- Adkin, Mark. 1989. *Urgent Fury: The Battle for Grenada: The Truth Behind the Largest U.S. Military Operation Since Vietnam.* Trans-Atlantic Publications. ISBN 0-85052-023-1
- Beck, Robert J. 1993. *The Grenada Invasion: Politics, Law, and Foreign Policy Decisionmaking.* Boulder: Westview Press. ISBN 0-8133-8709-4
- Brizan, George 1984. *Grenada Island of Conflict: From Amerindians to People's Revolution 1498–1979.* London, Zed Books Ltd., publisher; Copyright, George Brizan, 1984.
- Martin, John Angus. 2007. *A–Z of Grenada Heritage.* Macmillan Caribbean.
- Sinclair, Norma. 2003. *Grenada: Isle of Spice (Caribbean Guides).* Interlink Publishing Group; 3rd edition. ISBN 0-333-96806-9
- Stark, James H. 1897. *Stark's Guide-Book and History of Trinidad including Tobago, Grenada, and St. Vincent; also a trip up the Orinoco and a description of the great Venezuelan Pitch Lake.* Boston, James H. Stark, publisher; London, Sampson Low, Marston & Company.
- Steele, Beverley A. 2003. *Grenada: A History of Its People (Island Histories).* MacMillan Caribbean. ISBN 0-333-93053-3

External links

- Official Website of the Government of Grenada [3]
- Chief of State and Cabinet Members [4]
- Grenada [5] entry at *The World Factbook*
- Grenada [6] at *UCB Libraries GovPubs*
- Grenada [7] at the Open Directory Project
- Wikimedia Atlas of Grenada
- Grenada travel guide from Wikitravel
- Rural poverty in Grenada [8] (IFAD)
- grenadaisland.com [9]
- [10]
- The Grenada Revolution online [11]
- Brief History of Grenada [12]
- Presentation Brothers College [13]
- The Lost Bishop Photos [14]
- The evolution of class forces in Grenada [15]

1. REDIRECT Template:Navboxes

pnb:گرینیڈا

History of Grenada

Early History

About 2 million years ago Grenada was formed as an underwater volcano. Before the arrival of Europeans, Grenada, was inhabited by Carib Indians who had driven the more peaceful Arawaks from the island. Columbus sighted Grenada in 1498 during his third voyage to the new world. He named the island "Concepcion." The origin of the name "Grenada" is obscure, but it is likely that Spanish sailors renamed the island for the city of Granada. By the beginning of the 18th century, the name "Grenada", or "la Grenade" in French, was in common use. In 1609 the British was settle in Grenada. Partly because of the Caribs, Grenada remained uncolonized for more than one hundred years after its discovery; early English efforts to settle the island were unsuccessful. In 1650, a French company founded by Cardinal Richelieu purchased Grenada from the English and established a small settlement. After several skirmishes with the Caribs, the French brought in reinforcements from Martinique and defeated the Caribs, the last of whom leapt into the sea rather than surrender.

18th century

In 1705 The French began building Fort George as Fort Royal on St George's but it was completed by the British in 1710. The island remained under French control until its capture by the British in 1762, during the Seven Years' War. Grenada was formally ceded to the Kingdom of Great Britain by the Treaty of Paris (1763). Although the French regained control during the American War of Independence , winning the Battle of Grenada in July 1779, the island was restored to Britain with the Treaty of Versailles (1783). Although Britain was hard pressed to overcome a pro-French revolt in 1795, Grenada remained British for the remainder of the colonial period.

During the 18th century, Grenada's economy underwent an important transition. Like much of the rest of the West Indies, it was originally settled to cultivate sugar, which was grown on estates using slave labour from Africa. But natural disasters paved the way for the introduction of other crops. In 1782, Sir Joseph Banks, the botanical adviser to King George III, introduced nutmeg to Grenada. The island's soil was ideal for growing the spice and because Grenada was a closer source of spices for Europe than the Dutch East Indies, the island assumed a new importance to European traders.

19th century

The collapse of the sugar estates and the introduction of nutmeg and cocoa encouraged the development of smaller land holdings, and the island developed a land-owning yeoman farmer class. Slavery was outlawed in 1834. In 1833, Grenada became part of the British Windward Islands Administration. The governor of the Windward Islands administered the island for the rest of the colonial period. On the 3rd of December 1882, the largest wooden Jetty ever built in Grenada,was opened and took place in Gouyave. In 1895 the 340 foot Sendall Tunnel was built for horse carriages.

20th century and independence

On September the 22nd 1955 Hurricane Janet hit Grenada and 500 people were killed and 75% of the nutmeg trees of Grenada were destroyed. In 1958, the Windward Islands Administration was dissolved, and Grenada joined the Federation of the West Indies. After that federation collapsed in 1962, the British Government tried to form a small federation out of its remaining dependencies in the Eastern Caribbean.

Following the failure of this second effort, the British and the islanders developed the concept of "associated statehood". Under the Associated Statehood Act in 1967 Grenada was granted full autonomy over its internal affairs and was gained partial independence from Britain on the 3rd of March of that year. Full independence was granted on February 7, 1974.

After obtaining independence, Grenada adopted a modified Westminster parliamentary system based on the British model with a governor general appointed by and representing the British monarch (head of state) and a prime minister who is both leader of the majority party and the head of government. Sir Eric Gairy was Grenada's first prime minister.

Revolution and US invasion

On March 13, 1979, the New Jewel Movement launched an armed revolution which removed Gairy, suspended the constitution, and established a People's Revolutionary Government (PRG), headed by Maurice Bishop who declared himself prime minister. His Marxist-Leninist government established close ties with Cuba, Nicaragua, and other communist bloc countries. All political parties except for the New Jewel Movement were banned and no elections were held during the four years of PRG rule.

In October 1983, a power struggle within the government resulted in the illegal house arrest of Bishop at the order of his Deputy Prime Minister, Bernard Coard. Bishop's removal from office resulted in demonstrations in various parts of the island which eventually led to Bishop ceasing to be under house arrest. Coard's forces eventually executed Bishop and seven others including members of the cabinet.

After Bishop's death the military under Hudson Austin took power and formed a military government to run the country. A four-day total curfew was declared under which any civilian outside their home was subject to summary execution. A U.S.-Caribbean force landed on Grenada on October 25, 1983 in an action called *Operation Urgent Fury*. This action was taken in response to an appeal obtained from the governor general and to a request for assistance from the Organization of Eastern Caribbean States, without consulting the island's head of state, Queen Elizabeth II, Commonwealth institutions or other usual diplomatic channels (as had been done in Anguilla). Furthermore, United States government military strategists feared that Soviet use of the island would enable the Soviet Union to project tactical power over the entire Caribbean region. U.S. citizens were evacuated, and constitutional government was resumed.

Seventeen members of the PRG and the PRA (army) were convicted by a court. Fourteen were sentenced to death for actions related to the overthrow of the Bishop government and the murder of several persons including Bishop. The sentences were eventually commuted to life imprisonment after an international campaign. Another three were sentenced to forty five years in prison. These seventeen have become known as the Grenada 17, and are the subject of an ongoing international campaign for their release. In October 2003 Amnesty International issued a report which stated that their trial had been a miscarriage of justice. The seventeen have protested their sentences consistently since 1983.

After the invasion, United States gave $48.4 million in economic assistance to Grenada in 1984.

An advisory council named by the governor general administered the country until general elections were held in December 1984. The New National Party (NNP) led by Herbert Blaize won fourteen out of fifteen seats in elections and formed a democratic government. Grenada's constitution had been suspended in 1979 by the PRG but it was restored after the 1984 elections.

Late 20th century

The NNP continued in power until 1989 but with a reduced majority. Five NNP parliamentary members, including two cabinet ministers, left the party in 1986-87 and formed the National Democratic Congress (NDC) which became the official opposition.

In August 1989, Prime Minister Blaize broke with the NNP to form another new party, The National Party (TNP), from the ranks of the NNP. This split in the NNP resulted in the formation of a minority government until constitutionally scheduled elections in March 1990. Prime Minister Blaize died in December 1989 and was succeeded as prime minister by Ben Jones until after the elections.

The NDC emerged from the 1990 elections as the strongest party, winning seven of the fifteen available seats. Nicholas Brathwaite added two TNP members and one member of the Grenada United Labor Party (GULP) to create a 10-seat majority coalition. The governor general appointed him to be prime minister.

In parliamentary elections on June 20, 1995, the NNP won eight seats and formed a government headed by Dr. Keith Mitchell. The NNP maintained and affirmed its hold on power when it took all fifteen parliamentary seats in the January 1999 elections.

21st century

Truth and reconciliation commission

In 2000-2002 much of the controversy of the late 1970s and early 1980s was once again brought into the public consciousness with the opening of the truth and reconciliation commission. The commission was chaired by a Catholic priest, Father Mark Haynes, and was tasked with uncovering injustices arising from the PRA, Bishop's regime, and before. It held a number of hearings around the country. The commission was formed, bizarrely, because of a school project. Brother Robert Fanovich, head of Presentation Brothers' College (PBC) in St. George's tasked some of his senior students with conducting a research project into the era and specifically into the fact that Maurice Bishop's body was never discovered. Their project attracted a great deal of attention, including from the Miami Herald and the final report was published in a book written by the boys called *Big Sky, Little Bullet.* It also uncovered that there was still a lot of resentment in Grenadian society resulting from the era, and a feeling that there were many injustices still unaddressed. The commission began shortly after the boys concluded their project.

Hurricane Ivan

On September 7, 2004, Grenada was hit directly by category four Hurricane Ivan. The hurricane destroyed about 85% of the structures on the island, including the prison and the prime minister's residence, killed thirty nine people, and destroyed most of the nutmeg crop, Grenada's main economic mainstay. Grenada's economy was set back several years by Hurricane Ivan's impact. Hurricane Emily ravaged the island's north end in June 2005.

Further reading

- Kurlansky, Mark. 1992. *A Continent of Islands: Searching for the Caribbean Destiny.* Addison-Wesley Publishing. ISBN 0-201-52396-5.

External links

- Background Note: Grenada [1]
- History of Grenada [2]

Invasion of Grenada

Invasion of Grenada	
Part of the Cold War	

A U.S. Marine Corps Sikorsky CH-53D Sea Stallion helicopter hovers above the ground near a Soviet ZU-23 anti-aircraft weapon during the invasion

Date	October 25 – December 15, 1983
Location	Grenada
Result	United States/CPF victory

Belligerents	
United States **CPF:** Antigua and Barbuda Barbados Dominica Jamaica Saint Lucia Saint Vincent and the Grenadines	Grenada Cuba

Commanders and leaders	
Admiral Joseph Metcalf III H. Norman Schwarzkopf	Hudson Austin Pedro Tórtolo

Strength

United States: 7,300 infantry, marines, special forces **CPF:** 353 infantry, marines	**Grenada:** ~1,500 infantry, militia **Cuba:** 722 special forces, engineers
Casualties and losses	
United States: 19 killed, 116 wounded	**Grenada:** 45 killed, 358 wounded **Cuba:** 25 killed, 59 wounded, 638 captured
Civilian Casualties: 24 killed	

The **Invasion of Grenada**, codenamed **Operation Urgent Fury**, was a 1983 U.S.-led invasion of Grenada, a Caribbean island nation with a population of just over 100,000 located 100 miles (160 km) north of Venezuela. It was triggered by a military coup which ousted a brief revolutionary government. The successful invasion led to a change of government but was controversial due to charges of American imperialism, Cold War politics, the involvement of Cuba, the unstable state of the Grenadian government, and Grenada's status as a Commonwealth realm.

Grenada gained independence from the United Kingdom in 1974. Left wing rebels seized power in a coup in 1979. After a 1983 internal power struggle ended with the deposition and murder of revolutionary Prime Minister Maurice Bishop, the invasion began on October 25, 1983. A combined force of about 7,600 troops from the United States, Jamaica and members of the Regional Security System (RSS) defeated Grenadian resistance and the military government of Hudson Austin was deposed.

The invasion was criticized by the United Kingdom, Canada and the United Nations General Assembly, which condemned it as "a flagrant violation of international law". It enjoyed broad public support in the United States as well as in some sectors in Grenada who viewed the post-coup regime as illegitimate. October 25 is a national holiday in Grenada, called Thanksgiving Day, to commemorate this event. Additionally, on 29 May 2009, the Point Salines International Airport was officially renamed in honour of the slain pre-coup leader Maurice Bishop by the Government of Grenada.

Background

Sir Eric Gairy had led Grenada to independence from the United Kingdom in 1974. His term in office coincided with civil strife in Grenada. The political environment was highly charged and although Gairy – head of the Grenada United Labour Party – claimed victory in the general election of 1976, the opposition did not accept the result as legitimate. The civil strife took the form of street violence between government supporters and gangs organized by the New Jewel Movement. In the late 1970s, the NJM began planning to overthrow the government. Party members began to receive military training outside of Grenada. On March 13, 1979 while Gairy was out of the country, the NJM – led by Maurice Bishop – launched an armed revolution and overthrew the government, establishing the People's Revolutionary Government.

M102 howitzers firing during battle.

On October 13, 1983, a party faction led by Deputy Prime Minister Bernard Coard seized power. Bishop was placed under house arrest. Mass protests against the action led to Bishop escaping detention and reasserting his authority as the head of the government. Bishop was eventually captured and murdered along with several government officials loyal to him. The army under Hudson Austin then stepped in and formed a military council to rule the country. The Governor-General of Grenada, Paul Scoon, was placed under house arrest. The army announced a four-day total curfew where anyone seen on the streets would be subject to summary execution.

Members of the Eastern Caribbean Defense Force

After the United States invaded, Cuba released a series of official documents to the press. According to these documents, when the murder of Maurice Bishop was reported on October 20, the government of Cuba declared that it was "deeply embittered" by the murder and rendered "deep tribute" to the assassinated leader. The same official statement reported instructions to Cubans in Grenada that "they should abstain absolutely from any involvement in the internal affairs of the Party and of Grenada," while attempting to maintain the "technical and economic collaboration that could affect essential services and vital economic assistance for the Grenadian people."

American students waiting to be evacuated from the island

The Organisation of Eastern Caribbean States (OECS), then chaired by Eugenia Charles, the Prime Minister of Dominica; as well as the nations of Barbados, and Jamaica appealed to the United States for assistance. According to a reporter for *The New York Times*, this formal appeal was at the behest of the U.S. government, which had already decided to take military action. U.S. officials cited the murder of Bishop and general political instability in a country near U.S. borders, as well as the presence of U.S. medical students at St. George's University on Grenada, as reasons for military action. Sivapalan also claimed that the latter reason was cited in order to gain public support.

On October 22, 1983, Fidel Castro sent a public message to "Cuban workers" in Grenada, stressing that they should take no action in the event of a U.S. invasion unless they were "directly attacked." Referring to the Point Salines International Airport, the message ordered, if U.S. forces "land on the runway section near the university or on its surroundings to evacuate their citizens," Cubans were "to fully refrain from interfering."[*citation needed*]

On October 26, Alma Guillermoprieto reported in *The Washington Post* that at a "post-midnight news conference" with "almost 100 foreign and local journalists," Castro "released texts of what he said were diplomatic communications among Cuba, Grenada and the United States," giving the essential facts. U.S. sources "confirmed the exchange of messages," she added, but said they could not respond to Cuba at once because the telephone lines of the U.S. interest section in Havana were down from the evening of October 23 to late at night on October 24.

Reagan administration spokesman, Larry Speakes, said that "the U.S. disregarded Cuban and Grenadian assurances that U.S. citizens in Grenada would be safe because, 'it was a floating craps game and we didn't know who was in charge'." The same issue was reported by Alan Berger in *The Boston Globe* on the same day.

A Soviet-made BTR-60PB armored personnel carrier destroyed by Army Rangers on the afternoon of October 25, 1983 at the True Blue campus of the St. George's School of Medicine

Airport

The Bishop government began constructing the Point Salines International Airport with the help of Britain, Cuba, Libya, Algeria, and other nations.

The airport had been first proposed by the British government in 1954, when Grenada was still a British colony. It had been designed by Canadians, underwritten by the British government, and partly built by a London firm. The U.S. government accused Grenada of constructing facilities to aid a Soviet-Cuban military build-up in the Caribbean, and to assist the Soviet and Cuban transportation of weapons to Central American insurgents. Bishop's government claimed that the airport was built to accommodate commercial aircraft carrying tourists, pointing out that such jets could not land at the existing airport on the island's north. Neither could the existing airport, itself, be expanded as its runway abutted a mountain.

In 1982, then-Member of the United States House of Representatives Ron Dellums, traveled to Grenada on a fact-finding mission, having been invited by the country's Prime Minister. Dellums described his findings before Congress:

> ...based on my personal observations, discussion and analysis of the new international airport under construction in Grenada, it is my conclusion that this project is specifically now and has always been for the purpose of economic development and is not for military use.... It is my thought that it is absurd, patronizing and totally unwarranted for the United States Government to charge that this airport poses a military threat to the United States' national security.

In March 1983, Ronald Reagan began issuing warnings about the threat posed to the United States and the Caribbean by the "Soviet-Cuban militarization" as evidenced by the excessively long airplane runway being built as well as intelligence sources. He said that the 9000-foot (2700 m) runway and the oil storage tanks were unnecessary for commercial flights, and that evidence pointed that the airport was to become a Cuban-Soviet military airbase.

The invasion

The invasion, which commenced at 05:00 on October 25, 1983, was the first major operation conducted by the U.S. military since the Vietnam War.[citation needed]

An AH-1S firing its cannon.

Vice Admiral Joseph Metcalf, III, Commander Second Fleet, was the overall commander of the U.S. forces, designated Joint Task Force 120, which included elements of each military service and multiple special operations units.

Fighting continued for several days and the total number of U.S. troops reached some 7,000 along with 300 troops from the OECS. The invading forces encountered about 1,500 Grenadian soldiers and about 700 Cubans. Also present were 60 advisors from the Soviet Union, North Korea, East Germany, Bulgaria, and Libya.[citation needed]According to journalist Bob Woodward in his book "Veil", the supposed captured "military advisers" from the aforementioned countries were actually accredited diplomats and included their dependents. None took any actual part in the fighting. Some of the "construction workers" were actually a detachment of Cuban Military Special Forces and combat engineers.

Official U.S. sources state that the defenders were well-prepared, well-positioned and put up stubborn resistance, to the extent that the U.S. called in two battalions of reinforcements on the evening of October 26. The total naval and air superiority of the coalition forces — including helicopter gunships and naval gunfire support — overwhelmed the Communist forces.

> Nearly eight thousand soldiers, sailors, airmen, and Marines had participated in URGENT FURY along with 353 Caribbean allies of the CPF. U.S. forces had sustained 19 killed and 116 wounded; Cuban forces sustained 25 killed, 59 wounded and 638 combatants captured. Grenadian forces casualties were 45 killed and 358 wounded; at least 24 civilians were killed.

Reaction in the United States

A month after the invasion, *Time* magazine described it as having "broad popular support." A congressional study group concluded that the invasion had been justified, as most members felt that U.S. students at the university near a contested runway could have been taken hostage as U.S. diplomats in Iran had been four years previously. The group's report caused House Speaker Tip O'Neill to change his position on the issue from opposition to support.

However, some members of the study group dissented from its findings. Congressman Louis Stokes stated: "Not a single American child nor single American national was in any way placed in danger or placed in a hostage situation prior to the invasion." The Congressional Black Caucus denounced the invasion and seven Democratic congressmen, led by Ted Weiss, "introduced a quixotic resolution to impeach Reagan...which would, of course, go exactly nowhere."

In the evening of October 25, 1983 by telephone, on the newscast Nightline, anchor Ted Koppel spoke to medical students on Grenada who stated that they were safe and did not feel their lives were in danger. The next evening, again by telephone, medical students told Koppel how grateful they were for the invasion and the Marines, which probably saved their lives. State department officials had assured the medical students that they would be able to complete their medical school education in the United States.

International opposition and criticism

By a vote of 108 in favor to 9 (Antigua and Barbuda, Barbados, Dominica, El Salvador, Israel, Jamaica, Saint Lucia, Saint Vincent and the Grenadines, Grenada, and the United States voting against) with 27 abstentions, the United Nations General Assembly adopted General Assembly Resolution 38/7 which "deeply deplores the armed intervention in Grenada, which constitutes a flagrant violation of international law and of the independence, sovereignty and territorial integrity of that State". The government of China termed the United States intervention an outright act of hegemonism. The USSR government observed that Grenada had for a long time been the object of United States threats, that the invasion violated international law, and that no small nation not to the liking of the United States would find itself safe if the aggression against Grenada was not rebuffed. The governments of some countries stated that the United States intervention was a return to the era of barbarism. The governments of other countries said the United States by its invasion had violated several treaties and conventions to which it was a party.

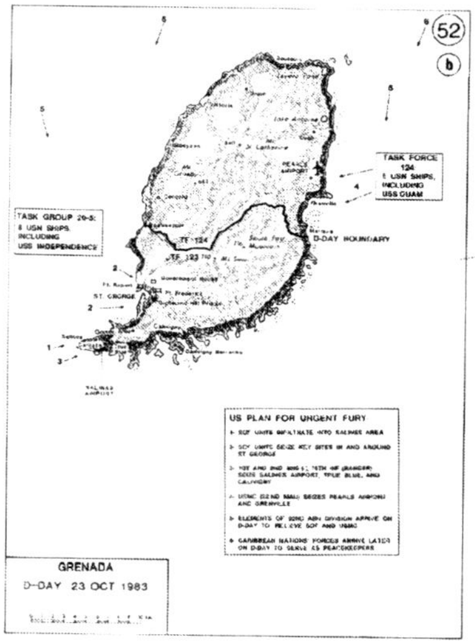

Map of invasion plan.

A similar resolution was discussed in the United Nations Security Council and although receiving widespread support it was ultimately vetoed by the United States. The then president of the United States Ronald Reagan, when asked if he was concerned by the lopsided 108-9 vote in the UN General Assembly said "it didn't upset my breakfast at all"

Grenada is part of the Commonwealth of Nations and, following the invasion, it requested help from other Commonwealth members. The invasion was opposed by the United Kingdom, Trinidad and Tobago, and Canada, among others. British Prime Minister Margaret Thatcher personally opposed the U.S. invasion, and her Foreign Secretary, Geoffrey Howe, announced to the British House of Commons on the day before the invasion that he had no knowledge of any possible U.S. intervention. Ronald Reagan, President of the United States, assured Thatcher that an invasion was not contemplated. Reagan later said, "She was very adamant and continued to insist that we cancel our landings on Grenada. I couldn't tell her that it had already begun."

After the invasion, Prime Minister Thatcher wrote to President Reagan: *This action will be seen as intervention by a Western country in the internal affairs of a small independent nation, however unattractive its regime. I ask you to consider this in the context of our wider East-West relations and of the fact that we will be having in the next few days to present to our Parliament and people the siting of Cruise missiles in this country...I cannot conceal that I am deeply disturbed by your latest communication.* The full text remains classified.

Aftermath

Following the U.S. victory, Grenada's Governor-General Paul Scoon formed a government. U.S. forces remained in Grenada after combat operations finished in December. Elements remaining included military police, special forces, and a specialized intelligence detachment.

A VA-87 A-7E from USS *Independence* over Port Salines airfield.

The invasion showed problems with the U.S. government's "information apparatus," which *Time* described as still being in "some disarray" three weeks after the invasion. For example, the U.S. State Department falsely claimed that a mass grave had been discovered that held 100 bodies of islanders who had been killed by Communist forces. Major General Norman Schwarzkopf, deputy commander of the invasion force, said that 160 Grenadian soldiers and 71 Cubans had been killed during the invasion; the Pentagon had given a much lower count of 59 Cuban and Grenadian deaths. Ronald H. Cole's report for the Joint Chiefs of Staff showed an even lower count.

Also of concern were the problems that the invasion showed with the military. There was a lack of intelligence about Grenada, which exacerbated the difficulties faced by the quickly assembled invasion force. For example, it was not known that the students were actually at two different campuses and there was a thirty-hour delay in reaching students at the second campus. Maps provided to soldiers on the ground were rudimentary, did not show topography, and were not marked with crucial positions. The U.S. Navy ships providing naval gunfire and U.S. Marine and Navy fighter bomber support, as well as U.S. Air Force aircraft providing close air support mistakenly fired upon and killed U.S. ground forces due to differences in maps and location coordinates, datum, and methods of calling for fire support. The landing strip was drawn-in by hand on the map given to some members of the invasion force.[citation needed]

Goldwater-Nichols Act

Main article: Goldwater–Nichols Act

Analysis by the U.S. Department of Defense showed a need for improved communications and coordination between the different branches of the U.S. forces. U.S. Congressional investigations of many of the reported problems resulted in the most important legislative change affecting the U.S. military organization, doctrine, career progression, and operating procedures since the end of World War II - the Goldwater-Nichols Department of Defense Reorganization Act of 1986 (Pub. L.99-433).

Calivigny barracks before and after being bombed.

The Goldwater-Nichols Act made the most sweeping changes to the United States Department of Defense since the department was established in the National Security Act of 1947. The Goldwater-Nichols Act reworked the command structure of the United States military. It increased the powers of the Chairman of the Joint Chiefs of Staff and created the concept of truly unified joint U.S. forces (i.e., Army, Air Force, Marines, and Navy forces organized under one command). One of the first reorganizations resulting from both the Department of Defense analysis and the legislation was the formation of the U.S. Special Operations Command in 1987.

Other

In 2008, the Government of Grenada announced a move to build a monument to honour the Cubans killed during the invasion. At the time of the announcement the Cuban and Grenadian government are still seeking to locate a suitable site for the monument.

A heavily fictionalized account of the invasion from a U.S. military perspective is shown in the 1986 Clint Eastwood movie, *Heartbreak Ridge*.

Order of battle

U.S. land forces

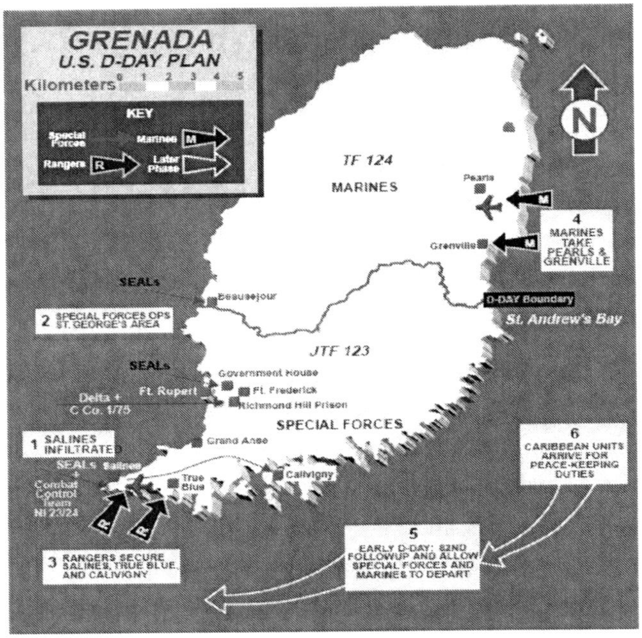

Operation Urgent Fury.

- 22nd Marine Amphibious Unit
- 82nd Airborne Division - large contingent
- 27th Engineer Battalion
- 21st Tactical Air Support Squadron - jump qualified FACs deployed with 82nd Airborne
- U.S. Air National Guard - provided A-7D Corsair II ground-attack aircraft for close air support
- 437th Military Airlift Wing - provided airlift support with C-141 Starlifters
- 16th Special Operations Wing - flew AC-130H Spectre gunships
- 33rd Tactical Fighter Wing - provided air superiority cover for allied forces with F-15 Eagles
- 75th Ranger Regiment - 1st and 2nd Battalions
- Navy SEALs: SEAL Team FOUR and SEAL Team SIX
- 1st Special Forces Operational Detachment-Delta
- E co 3/60th Inf Reg (later designated: E co 109th MI Battalion 9th ID LRSC (1984)
- 160th Special Operations Aviation Regiment (Airborne)
- 5th Weather Squadron, 5th Weather Wing (MAC) - Jump qualified Combat Weathermen who deployed with the 82nd
- 317th Military Airlift Wing - provided airlift support with Lockheed C-130 Hercules (Pope AFB NC)

U.S. naval forces

Amphibious Squadron Four USS *Guam* (LPH-9), USS *Barnstable County* (LST-1197), USS *Manitowoc* (LST-1180), USS *Fort Snelling* (LSD-30), USS *Trenton* (LPD-14)

Independence Task Group USS *Independence* (CV-62), USS *Richmond K. Turner* (CG-20), USS *Coontz* (DDG-40), USS *Caron* (DD-970), USS *Moosbrugger* (DD-980), USS *Clifton Sprague* (FFG-16), USS *Suribachi* (AE-21) with the Invasion Tactical Planning and Hands On Operational Control conducted by the Air Staff of the USS *Independence*

In addition, the following ships supported naval operations: USS *America* (CV-66), USS *Aquila* (PHM-4), USS *Aubrey Fitch* (FFG-34), USS *Briscoe* (DD-977), USS *Portsmouth* (SSN-707), USS *Recovery* (ARS-43), USS *Saipan* (LHA-2), USS *Sampson* (DDG-10), USS *Samuel Eliot Morison* (FFG-13), USS *Taurus* (PHM-3), and USCGC *Chase* (WHEC-718)

Caribbean Peace Force (CPF)

Notes

USS KIDD DDG-993 was relieved by the two PHMS 3 & 4 not sure why Kidd keeps getting cut out.

Further reading

- Stewart, Richard W.. *Operation Urgent Fury: The Invasion of Grenada, October 1983* [1]. United States Army Center of Military History. CMH Pub 70–114–1.
- Cole, Ronald H. (1997). *Operation Urgent Fury:The Planning and Execution of Joint Operations in Grenada, 12 October - 2 November 1983* [2].

External links

- Operation: Urgent Fury, Grenada [3]
- The 1983 Invasion of Grenada, Operation: Urgent Fury [4]
- A history of the operation from the U.S. perspective as written by naval historians. [5]
- *Grenada* [6] - a 1984 comic book about the invasion written by the CIA.
- NBC Nightly News report on day of Invasion of Grenada [7]

Geography of Grenada

Sobriquet: *The Spice Isle*

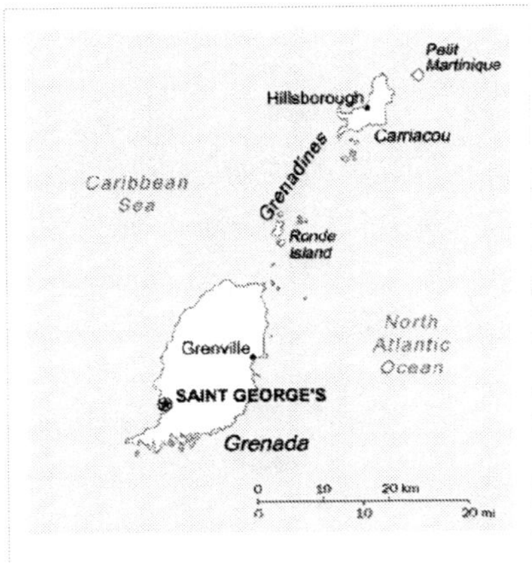

Map of Grenada

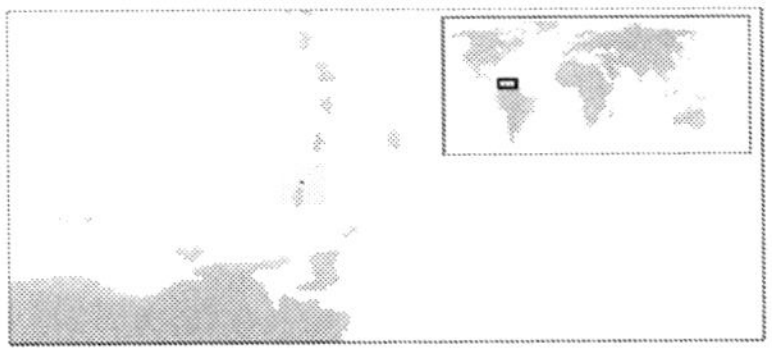

Geography	
Location	Caribbean Sea
Coordinates	12°07′N 61°40′W
Archipelago	Grenadines
Area	310 km^2 (120 sq mi)
Length	19 km (11.8 mi)
Width	34 km (21.1 mi)
Coastline	121 km (75.2 mi)
Highest elevation	840 m (2760 ft)
Highest point	Mount St. Catherine
Country	
Grenada	

Largest city	St. George's (pop. 7,500)
	Demographics
Population	110,000 (as of 2005)
Density	354.84 /km^2 (919.03 /sq mi)
Ethnic groups	Blacks 82% Mulatto 12% South Asians (Indo-Grenadians) 3% and whites 2.9%, trace Arawak/Carib Amerindian

This article describes the **geography of Grenada**.

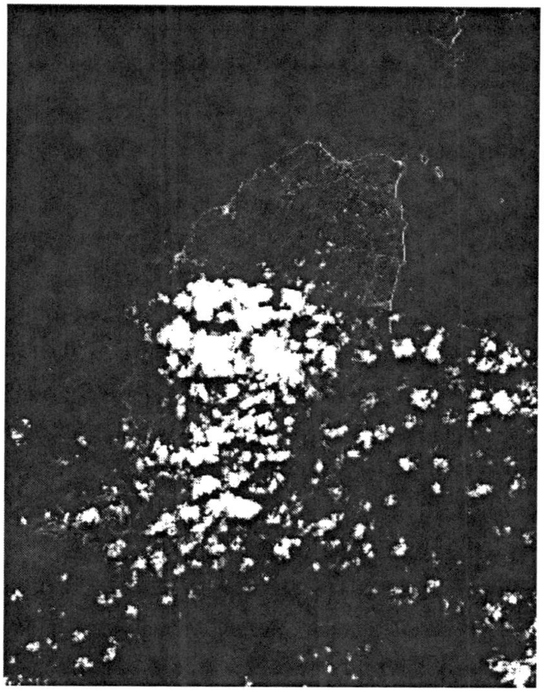

Grenada - NASA NLT Landsat 7 (Visible Color) Satellite Image

Grenada is a Caribbean island (one of the Grenadines) between the Caribbean Sea and Atlantic Ocean, north of Trinidad and Tobago. It is located at 12°07′N 61°40′W. There are no large inland bodies of water on the island, which consists entirely of the state of Grenada. The coastline is 121 km long.

Grenada has 15 constituencies and speaks English. It is volcanic in origin and its topography/land scape is mountainous.

Natural resources include timber, tropical fruit and deepwater harbors.

Grenada and its largely uninhabited outlying territories are the most southerly of the Windward Islands. The Grenadine Islands chain consists of some 600 islets; those south of the Martinique Channel belong to Grenada, while those north of the channel are part of the nation of St. Vincent and the Grenadines. Located about 160 kilometers north of Venezuela, at approximately 12° north latitude and 61° west longitude, Grenada and its territories occupy a total area of 433 square kilometers. Grenada, known as the Spice Isle because of its production of nutmeg and mace, is the largest at 310 square kilometers, or about the size of Detroit. The island is oval shape and framed by a jagged southern coastline; its maximum width is thirty-four kilometers, and its maximum length is nineteen kilometers. St. George's, the capital and the nation's most important harbor, is favorably situated near a lagoon on the southwestern coast. Of all the islands belonging to Grenada, only two are of consequence: Carriacou, with a population of a few thousand, and its neighbor Petit Martinique, roughly 40 kilometers northeast of Grenada and populated by some 700 inhabitants.

Part of the volcanic chain in the Lesser Antilles arc, Grenada and its possessions generally vary in elevation from under 300 meters to over 600 meters above sea level. Grenada is more rugged and densely foliated than its outlying possessions, but other geographical conditions are more similar. Grenada's landmass rises from a narrow, coastal plain in a generally north-south trending axis of ridges and narrow valleys. Mount St. Catherine is the highest peak at 840 meters.

Although many of the rocks and soils are of volcanic origin, the volcanic cones dotting Grenada are long dormant. Some of the drainage features on Grenada remain from its volcanic past. There are a few crater lakes, the largest of which is Grand Etang. The swift upper reaches of rivers, which occasionally overflow and cause flooding and landslides, generally cut deeply into the conic slopes. By contrast, many of the water courses in the lowlands tend to be sluggish and meandering.

Climate

The Grenadan climate is tropical, tempered by northeast trade winds. The land is volcanic in origin with mountains in the interior. The lowest point is at sea level, and the highest is 840 m (2756 ft) on Mount Saint Catherine.

The abundance of water is primarily caused by the tropical, wet climate. Yearly precipitation, largely generated by the warm and moisture-laden northeasterly trade winds, varies from more than 3500 millimeters (137.8 in) on the windward mountainsides to less than 1500 millimeters (59.1 in) in the lowlands. The greatest monthly totals are recorded throughout Grenada from June through November, the months when tropical storms and hurricanes are most likely to occur. Rainfall is less pronounced from December through May, when the equatorial low-pressure system moves south. Similarly, the highest humidities, usually close to 80 percent, are recorded during the rainy months, and values from 68 to 78 percent are registered during the drier period. Temperatures averaging 29 °C (84.2 °F) are constant throughout the year, however, with slightly higher readings in the lowlands. Nevertheless, diurnal ranges within a 24-hour period are appreciable: between 26 and 32 °C (78.8 and 89.6 °F) during the day and between 19 and 24 °C (66.2 and 75.2 °F) at night.

Statistics

Area

- Total: 340 km^2
- Land: 340 km^2

Maritime claims

- Exclusive economic zone: 200 nmi (370.4 km; 230.2 mi)
- Territorial sea: 12 nmi (22.2 km; 13.8 mi)

Land use

- Arable land: 15%

- Permanent crops: 18%
- Permanent pastures: 3%
- Forests and woodland: 9%
- Other: 55% (1993 est.)

Irrigated land

NA km²

Natural hazards

Lies on edge of hurricane belt; hurricane season lasts from June to November

Environment - current issues

NA

Environment - international agreements

Party to: Biodiversity, Climate Change, Desertification, Endangered Species, Law of the Sea, Ozone Layer Protection, Whaling

Geography - note

The administration of the islands of the Grenadines group is divided between Saint Vincent and the Grenadines (northern Grenadines) and Grenada (southern Grenadines)

References

- *This article incorporates public domain material from websites or documents* [1] *of the Library of Congress Country Studies.*
- *This article incorporates public domain material from websites or documents* [2] *of the CIA World Factbook.*

Politics of Grenada

Grenada

This article is part of the series:
Politics and government of Grenada

- Queen
  - Elizabeth II
- Governor-General
  - Carlyle Glean
- Prime Minister
  - Tillman Thomas
- Parliament
  - Senate
  - House of Representatives
- Political parties
- Elections: 2003, 2008
- Parishes
- Foreign relations

Other countries · Atlas
Politics portal

Politics of Grenada takes place in a framework of a parliamentary representative democratic monarchy, whereby the Prime Minister is the head of government, and of a multi-party system. Grenada is an independent country and Commonwealth Realm. It is a parliamentary democracy whose political and legal traditions closely follow those of the United Kingdom. Executive power is exercised by the government. Legislative power is vested in both the government and parliament. Constitutional safeguards include freedom of speech, press, worship, movement, and association. Grenada is a member of the eastern Caribbean court system. The Judiciary is independent of the executive and the legislature. Jurisprudence is based on English common law. Grenada is governed under a parliamentary system based on the British model; it has a governor general, a prime minister and a cabinet, and a bicameral Parliament with an elected House of Representatives and an appointed Senate.

Citizens enjoy a wide range of civil and political rights guaranteed by the constitution. Grenada's constitution provides citizens with the right to change their government peacefully. Citizens exercise this right through periodic, free, and fair elections held on the basis of universal suffrage.

Grenada has two significant political parties, both moderate: the National Democratic Congress (liberal) and the New National Party (conservative). Minor parties include the left-of-center Maurice Bishop Patriotic Movement (MBPM, organized by the pro-Bishop survivors of the October 1983 anti-Bishop coup) and the populist GULP of former Prime Minister Gairy.

At the July 2008 election the NDC won a comfortable 7 seat majority over the government of former Prime Minister Keith Mitchell. New Prime Minister Tillman Thomas formed a government after narrowly losing by one seat to Mitchell's NNP in the November 2003 election.

Security in Grenada is maintained by the 650 members of the Royal Grenada Police Force (RGPF), which included an 80-member paramilitary special services unit (SSU) and a 30-member coast guard. The U.S. Army and the U.S. Coast Guard provide periodic training and material support for the SSU and the coast guard.

Executive branch

As head of state, Queen Elizabeth II is represented in Grenada by a governor general who acts on the advice of the prime minister and the cabinet. The leader of the majority party serves as Prime Minister and head of government. The cabinet consists of members, including the Prime Minister and ministers of executive departments. They answer politically to the House of Assembly. The Governor General appoints the Chief Justice of the Supreme Court on the advice of the Prime Minister and the Leader of the Opposition. The Governor General appoints the other justices with the advice of a judicial commission. The Privy Council of the United Kingdom serves as the highest appellate court.Wikipedia:Disputed statement

Main office holders

Office	Name	Party	Since
Queen	Elizabeth II		6 February 1952
Governor-General	Carlyle Glean		27 November 2008
Prime Minister	Tillman Thomas	NDC	9 July 2008

Legislative branch

The Parliament has two chambers. The House of Representatives has 15 members, elected for a five year term in single-seat constituencies. The Senate has 13 appointed members, 10 appointed by the government and three by the leader of the opposition).

Political parties and elections

Summary of the 8 July 2008 Grenadan House of Representatives election results

Parties	**Votes**	**%**	**+/–**	**Seats**	**+/–**
National Democratic Congress	29,007	50.97	+5.4	11	+4
New National Party	27,189	47.77	–0.2	4	–4
Labour Platform	478	0.84	–2.4	—	±0
Good Ole Democracy	3	0.01	—	—	—
Independents	12	0.02	—	—	—
Invalid votes	222	0.39			—
Total (turnout 80.3%)	56,911	100.0		**15**	
Registered voters	70,869				
Source: Grenada Broadcast [1]					

House of Representatives of Grenada election results 2003

Parties	**Votes**	**%**	**+/-**	**Seats**	**+/-**
New National Party	22,566	48.0	-14.2	8	-7
National Democratic Congress	21,445	45.6	+20.7	7	+7
Grenada United Labour Party		3.2		-	
People's Labour Movement		2.2		-	
Total (turnout 57.4%)	47,239			**15**	
Invalid votes	249				
Total votes	47,488				
Registered voters	82,270				
Source: Adam Carr's Election Archive [2], IPU Parline and AFP					

Judicial branch

West Indies Associate States Supreme Court (an associate judge resides in Grenada)

Administrative divisions

6 parishes and 1 dependency*; Carriacou and Petit Martinique*, Saint Andrew, Saint David, Saint George, Saint John, Saint Mark, Saint Patrick

International organization participation

ACP, C, Caricom, CDB, ECLAC, FAO, G-77, IBRD, ICAO, ICFTU, ICRM, IDA, IFAD, IFC, IFRCS, ILO, IMF, IMO, Interpol, IOC, ISO (subscriber), ITU, LAES, NAM, OAS, OECS, OPANAL, OPCW, UN, UNCTAD, UNESCO, UNIDO, UPU, WCL, WHO, WIPO, WToO, WTrO,frat

Commonwealth realm

The Commonwealth realms, shown in blue. Former Commonwealth realms are shown in red.

A **Commonwealth realm** is a sovereign state within the Commonwealth of Nations that has Elizabeth II as its monarch and head of state. The sixteen current realms have a combined land area of 18.8 million km² (7.3 million mi², excluding Antarctic claims), and a population of 134 million; all but about two million live in the six most populous states, the United Kingdom, Canada, Australia, Papua New Guinea, New Zealand, and Jamaica.

Fourteen of the current and all former realms were once British colonies that evolved into independent states, the exceptions being the United Kingdom (UK) itself and Papua New Guinea, which was formed in 1975 as a union of the former German New Guinea — administered by Australia as an international trusteeship before independence — and the former British New Guinea — legally the territory of Papua, administered for the UK by Australia since 1905. The first realms to emerge were colonies that had already previously attained the status of a self-governing Dominion within the British

Empire. For a time, the older term of *Dominion* was retained to refer to these non-British realms, even though their actual status had changed with the granting of full legislative independence. The word is still sometimes used today, though increasingly rarely, as the word *realm* was formally introduced with the proclamation of Elizabeth II in 1952, and acquired legal status with the adoption of the modern royal styles and titles by the individual countries. The qualified term *Commonwealth realm* is not official, and has not been used in law; rather, it is a term of convenience for distinguishing this group of realms from other countries in the Commonwealth that do not share the same monarch.

Current Commonwealth realms

Country	Monarchy	Date	Queen's Title	Royal Standard
Antigua and Barbuda	Monarchy of Antigua and Barbuda	1981	Elizabeth the Second, by the Grace of God, Queen of Antigua and Barbuda and of Her other Realms and Territories, Head of the Commonwealth.	None
Australia	Monarchy of Australia	1942	Elizabeth the Second, by the Grace of God, Queen of Australia and Her other Realms and Territories, Head of the Commonwealth.	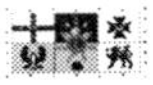
The Bahamas	Monarchy of the Bahamas	1973	Elizabeth the Second, by the Grace of God, Queen of the Commonwealth of the Bahamas and of Her other Realms and Territories, Head of the Commonwealth.	None
Barbados	Monarchy of Barbados	1966	Elizabeth the Second, by the Grace of God, Queen of Barbados and of Her other Realms and Territories, Head of the Commonwealth	
Belize	Monarchy of Belize	1981	Elizabeth the Second, by the Grace of God, Queen of Belize and of Her Other Realms and Territories, Head of the Commonwealth	None
Canada	Monarchy of Canada	1931	English: Elizabeth the Second, by the Grace of God, of the United Kingdom, Canada and Her other Realms and Territories Queen, Head of the Commonwealth, Defender of the Faith French: *Elizabeth Deux, par la grâce de Dieu Reine du Royaume-Uni, du Canada et de ses autres royaumes et territoires, Chef du Commonwealth, Défenseur de la Foi*	
Grenada	Monarchy of Grenada	1974	Elizabeth the Second, by the Grace of God, Queen of the United Kingdom of Great Britain and Northern Ireland and of Grenada and Her other Realms and Territories, Head of the Commonwealth	None
Jamaica	Monarchy of Jamaica	1962	Elizabeth the Second, by the Grace of God, Queen of Jamaica and of Her other Realms and Territories, Head of the Commonwealth	

New Zealand	Monarchy of New Zealand	1947	Elizabeth the Second, by the Grace of God, Queen of New Zealand and Her Other Realms and Territories, Head of the Commonwealth, Defender of the Faith	
Papua New Guinea	Monarchy of Papua New Guinea	1975	Elizabeth the Second, Queen of Papua New Guinea and of Her other Realms and Territories, Head of the Commonwealth	None
Saint Kitts and Nevis	Monarchy of Saint Kitts and Nevis	1983	Elizabeth the Second, by the Grace of God, Queen of Saint Christopher and Nevis and of Her other Realms and Territories, Head of the Commonwealth	None
Saint Lucia	Monarchy of Saint Lucia	1979	Elizabeth the Second, by the Grace of God, Queen of Saint Lucia and of Her other Realms and Territories, Head of the Commonwealth	None
Saint Vincent and the Grenadines	Monarchy of Saint Vincent and the Grenadines	1979	Elizabeth the Second, by the Grace of God, Queen of Saint Vincent and the Grenadines and of Her other Realms and Territories, Head of the Commonwealth	None
Solomon Islands	Monarchy of the Solomon Islands	1978	Elizabeth the Second, by the Grace of God, Queen of the Solomon Islands and of Her other Realms and Territories, Head of the Commonwealth	None
Tuvalu	Monarchy of Tuvalu	1978	Elizabeth the Second, by the Grace of God, Queen of Tuvalu and of Her other Realms and Territories, Head of the Commonwealth	None
United Kingdom	Monarchy of the United Kingdom	n/a	Elizabeth the Second, by the Grace of God, of the United Kingdom of Great Britain and Northern Ireland and of Her other Realms and Territories Queen, Head of the Commonwealth, Defender of the Faith	

Under the 1981 Cook Islands constitution, the Queen in Right of New Zealand is head of state of the Cook Islands, but no act passed by the Parliament of New Zealand after 1981 applies in the Cook Islands. For example, any change in the laws of succession to the New Zealand throne made by New Zealand would have no effect in the Cook Islands unless separately ratified there.

Relationship of the realms

The Commonwealth realms are sovereign states, united only in the voluntary and symmetric sharing of the institution of the monarchy, the succession, and the Queen herself. Terms such as *personal union*, a *form of personal union*, and *shared monarchy*, amongst others, have all been advanced as definitions since the beginning of the Commonwealth itself, though there has been no agreement on which term is most accurate, or even whether *personal union* is applicable at all. The United Kingdom no longer holds any legislative power over any country besides itself, although some countries continue to use, by their own volition, the Judicial Committee of the British Privy Council as part of their own judiciary;

usually as the highest court of appeal.

Potential or actual conflicts of interest have arisen from this relationship amongst independent states, ranging from minor diplomatic matters — such as the monarch expressing on the advice of one of her cabinets views that counter those of another of her cabinets — to more serious conflicts regarding matters of war, wherein the monarch may be simultaneously at war and at peace with himself as head of two hostile nations. In such cases, viceroys have tended to act in manners that avoid placing the sovereign directly in the centre of the conflict, meaning that a governor-general may have to take controversial actions entirely on his or her own initiative through the exercise of the reserve powers.

The Crown in the Commonwealth realms

The evolution of the Commonwealth realms has led to the scenario wherein the Crown has both a separate and a shared character; it is a singular institution with one sovereign, but also simultaneously operates separately within the jurisdiction of each country, with the Queen in right of a particular realm being a distinct legal person who acts only on the advice of the Cabinet of that state. This means that in different contexts the term *Crown* may refer to the extra-national institution shared amongst all 16 countries, or to the Crown in each realm considered separately. However, though the monarchy is therefore no longer an exclusively British institution, having become "domesticated" in each of the realms, for reasons historical, of convenience, or political it may in the media and legal fields often still be elaborated as the *British Crown*, regardless of the different, specific, and official national titles and terms used when addressing the Queen of the citizenry in each jurisdiction; for example, in Barbados the Queen is titled as *Elizabeth II, Queen of Barbados*, or simply the *Queen of Barbados*, with her full title making mention of her position as queen of the other Commonwealth realms. To guarantee the continuity of this arrangement, the preamble of the 1931 Statute of Westminster stipulates that any alteration to the line of succession in any one country must be voluntarily approved by the parliaments of all the realms, or, alternately, a realm may choose to end its participation in the shared monarchy.

From a cultural standpoint, the shared nature of the Crown is less clear. In all realms, the sovereign's name and image and other royal symbols unique to each nation are visible in the emblems and insignia of governmental institutions and militia, leading to the argument that the Crown as a shared link between the Commonwealth realms, with the Crown in right of each country having unique domestic characteristics. The Queen's effigy, for example, appears on coins and banknotes in some countries, and an oath of allegiance to the Queen is usually required from politicians, judges, military members and new citizens. It is also asserted, however, that the Crown throughout the realms remains essentially British and primarily of the United Kingdom, despite the legal and cultural evolution of the Commonwealth since the 1930s. Indeed, by 1959 it was being asserted by Buckingham Palace officials that the Queen was "equally at home in all her realms."

Monarch's role in the realms

The monarch is, in theory, the supreme governor of each of the Commonwealth realms, charged with issuing executive orders, commanding the military forces, and creating and administering laws. However, each country now operates under the Westminster system of parliamentary democracy and the concept of responsible government, meaning that the monarch only exercises her powers on the advice of her Crown ministers, who are usually drawn from, and thus responsible to, the elected lower house of the relevant parliament.

While this remains the case for all the Commonwealth realms, their sovereign resides predominantly in her oldest realm, the United Kingdom, and thus carries out her duties there mostly in person. In the other realms, the Queen normally exercises only those powers related to the appointment of her viceroys (a governor-general in all cases, and a governor in each of the Australian states), usually on the advice of the prime minister of the country or state concerned, though this process may have additional requirements. In certain other cases, the extent to which varies from realm to realm, specific additional powers are reserved exclusively for the monarch — such as the appointment of extra senators to the Canadian Senate, the creation of honours, or the issuance of letters patent — and on occasions of national importance, the Queen may be advised to perform in person her constitutional duties, such as granting Royal Assent or issuing a royal proclamation. Otherwise, all royal powers, including the Royal Prerogative, are carried out on behalf of the sovereign by the relevant viceroy, which, apart from those already mentioned, include a lieutenant governor in each province of Canada (appointed by the Governor General of Canada) and the Queen's Representative in the Cook Islands, who is appointed by the Queen herself. In the United Kingdom, the Queen appoints Counsellors of State to perform her constitutional duties in her absence.

Similarly, the monarch or other members of the Royal Family will perform ceremonial duties in the Commonwealth realms to mark historically significant events. They do so most frequently in the United Kingdom, and in the other countries during tours at least once every five or six years, meaning the Queen is present in a number of her dominions outside the UK, or acting on behalf of those realms abroad, approximately every other year.

Religious role of the monarch

The sovereign's religious role differs from country to country. In all realms except Papua New Guinea, the Queen is sovereign "By the Grace of God", a phrase that forms a part of her official title within those states. In Canada, the United Kingdom, and New Zealand, "Defender of the Faith" (in Latin: *fidei defensor*) — the ancient phrase first granted in 1521 by Pope Leo X to King Henry VIII — is also included as a part of the royal title and the sovereign is anointed as such in the only coronation that takes place in any of the realms, a ceremony in the context of a church service imbued with theological and constitutional symbolism and meaning, held at Westminster Abbey in London, United Kingdom.

However, as no realm other than the UK (England and Scotland only) has an established church, it is only there that the Queen actually plays a direct role in organised religion, acting not only as the Supreme Governor of the Church of England — appointing for it bishops and archbishops who thereafter act as her Lords Spiritual — but also sitting as an ordinary member of the Church of Scotland, albeit one who swears an oath to uphold and protect the church and sends to meetings of the church's General Assembly a Lord High Commissioner as her representative, when she is not personally in attendance. Unusually for the Church of Scotland, Glasgow and Dunblane Cathedrals are both owned by the British Crown, though they are not like the Chapels Royal, which exist in both the United Kingdom and Canada and form a part of the Ecclesiastical Household in those two countries. In England and Scotland, these chapels are known as Royal Peculiars, and fall directly within the jurisdiction of the British monarch, as opposed to a diocese, as is the norm. To them, the Queen may also appoint her own chaplains from either the Church of England or of Scotland.

Royal family

As with the sovereign, a single royal family is shared by the Commonwealth realms, similarly being most frequently referred to in a casual fashion as the *British Royal Family*, sometimes causing conflict with official national titles, such as in Canada. Though there is no strict legal or formal definition of who is or is not a member of the Royal Family, the group is loosely defined as the extended family of the monarch. These persons constitute the apex of a modern royal court, regularly performing public duties at hundreds of events throughout the 16 realms each year. For this work, the Royal Family members receive no salary from any state; instead, only the expenses incurred for each event (security, transportation, venue, etc.) are, due to the nature of the Crown in the realms, funded by the relevant state individually through the ordinary legislative budgeting process. These engagements are organised in order for the Crown to honour, encourage, and learn about the achievements or endeavours of individuals, institutions, and enterprises in a variety of areas of the lives of the Queen's subjects. As representatives of the monarch, Royal Family members often also join the nation in commemorating historical events, holidays, and celebratory and tragic occurrences, as well as sponsoring or participating in numerous charitable, cultural, and social activities. Their work, which is all formally recorded in the Court Circular, draws public attention to amicable relations within and between the nations of the Commonwealth and beyond; the members of the Royal Family draw enormous media coverage in the form of photographic, written, and televised commentary on not only their activities and public roles, but also family relationships, rites of passage, personalities, attire, and behaviour.

Flags

The Personal Flag of Queen Elizabeth II, used in a general capacity within the Commonwealth

The Queen employs various royal standards to mark her presence, the particular one used depending on which realm she is in or acting on behalf of at the time. There are currently unique flags for Australia, Barbados, Canada, Jamaica, New Zealand, and two variations for the United Kingdom — one for Scotland and another for the rest of the country. All are heraldic banners displaying the shield of the sovereign's coat of arms for that state, and each, save for those of the UK, are defaced in the centre with the Queen's Personal Flag, a crowned *E* for *Elizabeth* surrounded by a garland of roses representing the countries of the Commonwealth. This latter flag on its own is used for realms that do not have a unique personal standard for the monarch, as well as for general use in representing the Queen as Head of the Commonwealth. The monarch previously held royal standards for Sierra Leone, Mauritius, Malta, and Trinidad and Tobago, but these banners became obsolete when the countries became republics.

The governors-general throughout the Commonwealth realms also each use a personal flag, which, like that of the sovereign, passes to each successive occupant of the office. Most feature a lion passant atop a St. Edward's royal crown with the name of the country across a scroll underneath, all on a blue background. The two exceptions are those of, since 1981, Canada (bearing on a blue background the crest of the Royal Coat of Arms of Canada) and, since 2008, New Zealand (a St. Edward's Crown above the shield of the Coat of Arms of New Zealand). The lieutenant governors of the Canadian provinces each have their own personal standards, as do the governors of the Australian states.

Historical development

Dominions emerge

The possibility that a colony within the British Empire might become a new kingdom was first mooted in the 1860s, when it was proposed that the British North American territories of Nova Scotia, New Brunswick, and the Province of Canada unite as a confederation that might be known as the *Kingdom of Canada*. In light of geo-political circumstances at the time, however, the name was abandoned in favour of the *Dominion of Canada*. As more British colonies followed Canada in gaining legislative independence from the United Kingdom, Prime Minister of Canada Wilfrid Laurier was led to insist at the 1907 Imperial Conference that a formula be created to differentiate between the Crown and the self-governing colonies. For the latter the Canadian precedent was followed, and the term *Dominion* was extended to apply to Australia, New Zealand, Newfoundland, and the colonies of the Cape, Natal, and Transvaal, before and after they merged in 1910 with the Orange River Colony to form the Union of South Africa. These countries were joined in 1921 by the Irish Free State.

A compiled portrait of the main delegates to the signing of the Treaty of Versailles; Prime Minister of Canada Robert Borden sits fourth from left

King George V with his prime ministers at the Imperial Conference of 1926

Although the Dominions were capable of governing themselves internally, they technically remained — especially in regards to foreign policy and defence — subject to British authority, wherein the governor-general of each Dominion represented the British monarch-in-Council reigning over these territories as a single imperial domain. It was commonly held in some circles that the Crown was a monolithic element throughout all the monarch's territories; A.H. Lefroy wrote in 1918 that "the Crown is to be considered as one and indivisible throughout the Empire; and cannot be severed into as many kingships as there are Dominions, and self-governing colonies." This unitary model began to erode, however, when the Dominions gained more international prominence as a result of their participation and sacrifice in the First World War, in 1919 prompting Canadian prime minister Robert Borden and South African minister of defence Jan Smuts to demand that the Dominions be given at the Versailles Conference full recognition as "autonomous nations of an Imperial Commonwealth." The immediate result was that, though the King signed as High Contracting Party for the empire as a whole, the Dominions were also separate signatories to the Treaty of Versailles, as well as, together with India, founding members of the League of Nations. The pace of independence thereafter increased, with Canada exchanging envoys with the United States the following year and in 1923 concluding in its own right the Halibut Fisheries Treaty, Prime Minister of the United Kingdom David Lloyd George stating in 1921 that the "British Dominions have now been accepted fully into the community of nations," and, by 1925, the Dominions felt confident enough to refuse to be bound by Britain's adherence to the Treaty of Locarno. This, combined with a realisation that the Crown was already operating distinctly and separately within each of the jurisdictions of the Canadian provinces and Australian states, appeared to put to rest previous assertions that the Crown could never be divided amongst the Dominions.

Between the wars

Another catalyst for change came in 1926, when then Governor General of Canada the Lord Byng of Vimy refused the advice of his prime minister (William Lyon Mackenzie King) in what came to be known colloquially as the King-Byng Affair. Mackenzie King, after being dismissed and then reappointed as prime minister some months later, pushed at the Imperial Conference of 1926 for a reorganisation of the way the Dominions related to the British government, resulting in the Balfour Declaration, which declared formally that the Dominions were fully autonomous and equal in status to the United Kingdom. What this meant in practice was not at the time worked out; conflicting views existed at the time, some in the United Kingdom not wishing to see a fracturing of the sacred unity of the Crown throughout the empire, and some in the Dominions not wishing to see their jurisdiction have to take on the full brunt of diplomatic and military responsibilities.

What did follow was that the Dominion governments gained a separate and direct relationship with the monarch, without the British Cabinet acting as an intermediary, and the governors-general now acted solely as a personal representative of the sovereign in right of that Dominion. Though no formal mechanism for tendering advice to the monarch had yet been established — former Prime Minister of Australia William Hughes theorised that the Dominion cabinets would provide informal direction and the British Cabinet would offer formal advice — the concepts were first put into legal practice with the passage in 1927 of the Royal and Parliamentary Titles Act, which implicitly recognised the Irish Free State as separate from the UK, and the King as king *of* each Dominion uniquely, rather than as the British king *in* each Dominion. At the same time, terminology in foreign relations was altered to demonstrate the independent status of the Dominions, such as the dropping of the term "Britannic" from the King's style outside of the United Kingdom. Then, in 1930 George V's Australian ministers employed a practice adopted by resolution at that year's Imperial Conference, directly advising the King to appoint Isaac Isaacs as his Australian governor-general, against the preferences of the British government.

These new developments were explicitly codified in 1931 with the passage of the Statute of Westminster, through which Canada, the Union of South Africa, and the Irish Free State all immediately obtained formal legislative independence from the UK, while in the other Dominions' adoption of the statute was subject to ratification by the Dominion's parliament. Australia and New Zealand did so in 1942 and 1947, respectively, with the former's ratification back-dated to 1939, and, though originally covered by it, Newfoundland never ratified the bill and reverted to direct British rule in 1934. What resulted was the inability for the parliament at Westminster to legislate for any Dominion unless requested to do so. Further, the Judicial Committee of the British Privy Council was left available as the last court of appeal for some Dominions. This was all met with only minor trepidation either before or at the time, and the government of Ireland was confident that the relationship of these independent countries under the Crown would function as a personal union, akin to that which had earlier existed between the United Kingdom and Hanover (1801 to 1837), or between

England and Scotland (1603 to 1707). The civil division of the Court of Appeal of England and Wales later found in 1982 that the British parliament could have legislated for a Dominion simply by including in any new law a clause claiming the Dominion cabinet had requested and approved of the act, whether that was true or not. Further, the British parliament was not obliged to fulfill a Dominion's request for legislative change. However, the words in the Statute of Westminster became written expression of a conventional rule that developed whereby British law would not extend beyond the borders of the United Kingdom unless a Dominion supplicated otherwise. By 1937, the Appeal Division of the Supreme Court of South Africa ruled unanimously that a repeal of the Statute of Westminster in the United Kingdom would have no effect in South Africa, stating: "We cannot take this argument seriously. Freedom once conferred cannot be revoked." Others in Canada upheld the same position.

The first prominent example of this arrangement working in practice came with the abdication of King Edward VIII in 1936, for which it was necessary to gain the approval of all the Dominions of the Commonwealth before the resignation could take place; Canada, the Union of South Africa, and the Irish Free State even passed unique legislation to solidify the changes in succession within their jurisdictions. Following the accession of Edward's brother, George VI, to the throne, the United Kingdom created legislation that would provide for a regency in the event of the incapacitation of the monarch. Though input was sought from the Dominions on this matter, all declined to make themselves bound by the British legislation, feeling instead that the governors-general could carry out royal functions in place of a debilitated sovereign.

The prime ministers of five Commonwealth countries at the 1944 Commonwealth Prime Ministers' Conference; from left to right: William Lyon Mackenzie King (Canada), Jan Smuts (South Africa), Winston Churchill (United Kingdom), Peter Fraser (New Zealand), and John Curtin (Australia)

During his tenure as Governor General of Canada, the Lord Tweedsmuir urged the organisation of a royal tour of the country by King George VI, so that he might not only appear in person before his people, but also personally perform constitutional duties and pay a state visit to the United States as king of Canada. While the idea was embraced in Canada as a way to "translate the Statute of Westminster into the actualities of a tour," throughout the planning of the trip that took place in 1939, the British authorities resisted at numerous points the idea that the King be attended by his Canadian ministers instead of his British ones. The Canadian prime minister (still Mackenzie King) was ultimately successful, however, in being the minister in attendance, and the King did in public throughout the trip ultimately act solely in his capacity as the Canadian monarch. Yet, the international status of the Crown was also illustrated by George VI simultaneously bolstering from both Canada and the United States support for the UK in the looming war with Nazi Germany.

When this threat became reality, there was some uncertainty in the Dominions about the ramifications of Britain's declaration of war against Adolf Hitler. Australia and New Zealand had not yet ratified the Statute of Westminster; the Australian prime minister, Robert Menzies, considered the government bound by the British declaration of war, while New Zealand coordinated a declaration of war to be made simultaneously with Britain's. As late as 1937, some scholars were still of the mind that, when it came to declarations of war, if the King signed, he did so as king of the empire as a whole; at that time, W. Kennedy wrote: "in the final test of sovereignty — that of war — Canada is not a sovereign state... and it remains as true in 1937 as it was in 1914 that when the Crown is at war, Canada is legally at war," and, one year later, A. Berriedale Keith argued that "issues of war or neutrality still are decided on the final authority of the British Cabinet." In 1939, however, Canada and South Africa made separate proclamations of war against Germany a few days after the UK's. Their example was followed more consistently by the other realms as further war was declared against Italy, Rumania, Hungary, Finland, and Japan. At the war's end, it was said by F.R. Scott that "it is firmly established as a basic constitutional principle that, so far as relates to Canada, the King is regulated by Canadian law and must act only on the advice and responsibility of Canadian ministers."

Post-war evolution

Once the Second World War was over, India, Pakistan, and Ceylon became independent Dominions of the Commonwealth, though it was made clear at the time that India would soon move to a republican form of government. Unlike Ireland and Burma at the time of their becoming republics, however, there was no desire on the part of India to give up its membership in the British Commonwealth, prompting a Commonwealth Conference and the issuance of the London Declaration in 1949, which entrenched the idea of Canadian prime minister Louis St. Laurent that different royal houses and republics be allowed in the Commonwealth so long as they recognised as the international organisation's symbolic head the shared sovereign of the UK and the Dominions. At approximately the same time, the tabling in 1946 of the Canadian parliament's Canadian Citizenship Act brought into question the homogeneity of the King's subjects, which, prior to that year, was uniformly defined in terms of allegiance to the sovereign, without regard to the individual's country of residence. Following negotiations, it was decided in 1947 that each Commonwealth member was free to pass its own citizenship legislation, so that its citizens owed allegiance only to the monarch in right of that country.

As these constitutional developments were taking place, the Dominion and British governments became increasingly concerned with how to represent the more commonly accepted notion that there was no distinction between the sovereign's role in the UK and his or her position in any of the Dominions, as summed up in Patrick Gordon Walker's statement in the British House of Commons: "We in this country have to abandon... any sense of property in the Crown. The Queen, now, clearly, explicitly and according to title, belongs equally to all her realms and to the Commonwealth as a whole." Thus, at the 1948 Prime Ministers' Conference the term *Dominion* was avoided in favour of *Commonwealth country*, in order to avoid the subordination implied by the older designation. Then, with the British proclamation of Elizabeth II's accession to the throne in 1952, the phrases *Commonwealth realm* and *Head of the Commonwealth* became established, deriving from the words that declared the monarch as "of this Realm, and of her other Realms and Territories Queen, Head of the Commonwealth." The Commonwealth realms' prime ministers thereafter discussed the matter of the new monarch's title, with St. Laurent stating at the 1953 Commonwealth Conference that it was important to agree on a format that would "emphasise the fact that the Queen is Queen of Canada, regardless of her sovereignty over other Commonwealth countries." The result was a new Royal Style and Titles Act being passed in each of the seven realms then existing (excluding Pakistan), which all identically gave formal recognition to the separateness and equality of the countries involved, and replaced the phrase "British Dominions Beyond the Seas" with "Her Other Realms and Territories", the latter using the medieval French word *realm* (from *royaume*) in place of *dominion*. Further, at her coronation, Elizabeth II's oath contained a provision requiring her to promise to govern according to the rules and customs of the realms, naming each one separately.

The principle of fully separate and equal realms was followed in all future grants of independence, including those that came through the *winds of change* that swept through Africa in the 1960s, the collapse of the Federation of the West Indies in 1961, and at later dates. In post-colonial Africa, within a few years of their founding the realms drafted new constitutions in order to come under a different royal house or become republics within the Commonwealth; South Africa was the only exception, having been a Dominion and then a realm for 54 years before becoming a republic in 1961. The white minority government of Rhodesia in 1965 issued its unilateral declaration of independence, and its members affirmed their loyalty to Elizabeth II as *Queen of Rhodesia*, a title to which she had not consented, did not accept, and was not recognised internationally. Her representative in the colony, Sir Humphrey Gibbs, immediately dismissed his prime minister, Ian Smith, but this action was ignored by Smith and he appointed, without the Queen's consent, an Officer Administrating the Government to perform the governor's constitutional duties until 1970, when Smith's government declared Rhodesia a republic. When Papua New Guinea became independent of Australia in 1975, this was the first (and so far the last) time a Commonwealth realm was created from a territory that had never been made up of British colonies in its entirety. The country to most recently become a Commonwealth realm was Saint Kitts and Nevis, achieving the status in 1983. At the same time, in other Commonwealth realms, movements emerged to end their respective country's involvement in the shared monarchy, most advocating a republican government in place of constitutional monarchy; simultaneously, they were countered by monarchist leagues that support the existing system and celebrate the historical and modern connections the shared monarchy provides.

Queen Elizabeth II, on 6 July 2010, addressed the United Nations in New York City as queen of all 16 Commonwealth realms.

Former Commonwealth realms

Country	Dates	Original system	Method	Royal Standard
Ceylon	1948 – 1972	Parliamentary republic	New constitution	
Fiji	1970 – 1987	Parliamentary republic	Military coup	
Gambia	1965 – 1970	Presidential republic	Referendum	
Ghana	1957 – 1960	Presidential republic	Referendum	
Guyana	1966 – 1970	Parliamentary republic	Constitutional amendment	
India	1947 – 1950	Parliamentary republic	New constitution	
Ireland	1931 – 1949	Parliamentary republic	Act of parliament	
Kenya	1963 – 1964	Presidential republic	New constitution	
Malawi	1964 – 1966	Single-party republic	New constitution	
Malta	1964 – 1974	Parliamentary republic	Constitutional amendment	
Mauritius	1968 – 1992	Parliamentary republic	Constitutional amendment	
Nigeria	1960 – 1963	Parliamentary republic	Constitutional amendment	
Pakistan	1947 – 1956	Parliamentary republic	New constitution	
Sierra Leone	1961 – 1971	Presidential republic	New constitution	
South Africa	1931 – 1961	Parliamentary republic	Referendum	
Tanganyika	1961 – 1962	Presidential republic	New constitution	
Trinidad and Tobago	1962 – 1976	Parliamentary republic	New constitution	
Uganda	1962 – 1963	Parliamentary republic	Constitutional amendment	

Republican referendums

Various Commonwealth realms have held referendums to consider whether they should become republics. These include:

- Ghanaian constitutional referendum, 1960 (*passed*)
- South African republic referendum, 1960 (*passed*)
- Gambian republic referendum, 1965 (*failed: majority not 2/3*)
- Gambian republic referendum, 1970 (*passed*)
- Australian republic referendum, 1999 (*failed*)
- Tuvaluan constitutional referendum, 2008 (*failed*)
- Saint Vincent and the Grenadines constitutional referendum, 2009 (*failed*)

See also

- Commonwealth of Nations
- Commonwealth member states
- Commonwealth unification movement
- States headed by Elizabeth II
- Self-governing colony
- British overseas territories

Bibliography

- Bogdanor, V.; *The Monarchy and the Constitution*; Oxford: Oxford University Press; 1995
- Cox, Noel; "The Theory of Sovereignty and the Importance of the Crown in the Realms of The Queen"; *Oxford University Commonwealth Law Journal*; Vol. 2, No. 2; 2002
- Forsey, Eugene; *Royal Power of Dissolution on Parliament in the British Commonwealth*; Toronto: Oxford University Press; 1968 [1943]
- Maitland, F; "The Crown as a Corporation"; *Law Quarterly Review*; Vol. 17, No. 131; 1901
- McIntyre; P.; "The Strange Death of Dominion Status", *Journal of Imperial and Commonwealth History*; Vol. 27, No. 2; 1999; 193-212

Economy of Grenada

Economy of Grenada	

Currency	East Caribbean dollar (2.7 per US$ fixed rate since 1976)
Trade organisations	CARICOM
Statistics	
GDP	$360 million (2007 est.)
GDP growth	5% (1999 est.)
GDP per capita	$3,700 (1999 est.)
GDP by sector	agriculture: 9.7%; industry: 15%; services: 75.3% (est.)
Inflation (CPI)	-1.3% (1998 est.)
Labour force	42,300 (1996 est.)
Labour force by occupation	agriculture 24%, industry 14%, services 62% (1999 est.)
Unemployment	15% (1997 est.)
Main industries	food and beverages, textiles, light assembly operations, tourism, construction
Ease of Doing Business Rank	91st
External	
Exports	$26.8 million (1998 est.)
Export goods	bananas , cocoa , nutmeg , fruit and vegetables , clothing, mace
Main export partners	Caricom 4.2% , United Kingdom 20%, United States 13%, Netherlands 8.8% (1991)
Imports	$200 million (1998 est.)
Import goods	food, manufactured goods, machinery, chemicals, fuel (1989)
Main import partners	United States 31.2%, Caricom 23.6%, United Kingdom 13.8%, Japan 7.1% (1991)
Public finances	
Public debt	$89.2 million (1998)
Economic aid	$8.3 million (1995)

All values, unless otherwise stated, are in US dollars

Economic Overview

Grenada has a largely tourism-based, small, open economy. Over the past two decades, the economy has shifted from one of agriculture-dominant into that of services-dominant, with tourism serving as the leading foreign currency earning sector. The country's principal export crops are the spices nutmeg and mace (Grenada is the world's second largest producer of nutmeg after Indonesia). Other crops for export include cocoa, citrus fruits, bananas, cloves, and cinnamon. Manufacturing industries in Grenada operate mostly on a small scale, including production of beverages and other foodstuffs, textiles, and the assembly of electronic components for export.

Economic growth picked up in the late 1990s following slow growth and domestic fiscal adjustment in early years of the decade. Despite an expansionary fiscal policy, the public debt remained moderate at around 50 percent of GDP as deficits were financed partly by privatization receipts. Since 2001, economic growth declined caused by adverse shocks such as a slowdown in the global economy and natural disasters. To deal with the shocks, fiscal policy became more expansionary while privatization receipts declined. As a result, public debt increased sharply to near 110 percent of GDP in 2003. Economic conditions worsened when Hurricane Ivan hit the country in September 2004; progress in fiscal consolidation was impeded as government revenues fell and policy priority was shifted to post-hurricane relief.

Although reconstruction has proceeded quickly with significant aid from the international community, tourism and agricultural activities remain weak and nearly offset the stimulus from the reconstruction boom. The country is still facing the difficult task of reconstruction and recovery, while public debt is unsustainable and the government faces large financing gaps. In the years ahead, reinvigorating growth will be a high priority, and continued efforts are needed to address vulnerabilities.

Economic Performance

After experiencing GDP growth averaging nearly six percent a year in the late 1990s, economic growth declined considerably after 2001 as a result of a decline in the tourism industry following the September 11, 2001, terrorist attacks, and damages caused by several hurricanes.

The economy of Grenada was brought to a near standstill in September 2004 by Hurricane Ivan, which damaged or destroyed 90 percent of the country's buildings, including some tourist facilities. In July 2005 Hurricane Emily struck Grenada again as the country was still recovering from the impact of Hurricane Ivan. Besides the negative impacts to the tourism industry, the two devastating hurricanes destroyed or significantly damaged a large percentage of Grenada's tree crops, which may take years to recover.

As the damage of Hurricane Ivan to the economy exceeded 200 percent of GDP, economic growth registered a negative growth of three percent in 2004, compared with a positive growth rate of 5.8 percent in 2003. Although signs of recovery have been seen in Grenada after the damage inflicted by Hurricanes Ivan and Emily, economic conditions remain difficult; GDP is projected at a growth rate of only one percent for 2005.

With the absence of sustained growth, the fiscal situation started to deteriorate after 2001 reflecting a continued expansionary policy with sharp increase in spending on social sectors, the wage bill, and goods and services. As a result, the fiscal deficit rose to 8.5 percent of GDP in 2001 from 3.2 percent in 2000. The fiscal situation remained shaky in 2002 with the deficit widening to 19.2 percent of GDP due to dampened output from Tropical Storm Lili. As the economic began to recover in 2003, the government began to take steps for fiscal consolidation, and the fiscal deficit fell to 4.8 percent of GDP. But progress in fiscal consolidation was impeded in 2004 as the government policy changed abruptly to post-hurricane relief. Meanwhile, government revenues decreased as a result of the impact of the hurricanes on the economy.

While economic growth has declined since 2001 due to adverse shocks, including slowdown in the global economy and natural disasters, fiscal policy became more expansionary when privatization receipts declined. As a result, public debt has increased sharply to over 100 percent of GDP since 2002; it remained as high as near 130 percent of GDP in 2004.

Grenada is a member of the Eastern Caribbean Central Bank (ECCB), which manages monetary policy and issues a common currency for all the member countries. Inflation has remained low and stable within the framework of the currency board arrangement, with inflation averaging at two percent over the past 15 years.

Balance of Payments

Grenada's current account balance has remained in large deficit due to its heavy dependence on import of most consumer goods and domestic investment. Following an average deficit of around 20 percent of GDP from 1997 to 2000, the current account deficit has increased to over 30 percent of GDP since 2001 due to higher import demand combined with lower receipts from tourism and nutmeg exports. The current account deficits are financed by inflows of foreign direct investment, official grants and loans, and commercial borrowing by the private sector.

Grenada's economy is vulnerable to external shocks considering its high dependence on tourism, exports, and imports of most of the goods that are consumed or invested domestically. It is also prone to other adverse shocks such as natural disasters.

Regional Situation

In the aftermath of Hurricanes Ivan and Emily, the priority now for Grenada is to continue the recovery process necessary to restore the infrastructure that was devastated by the hurricanes. The international community has disbursed significant amounts of aid, including financial help under the International Monetary Fund's emergency assistance policy for natural disasters and assistance from the World Bank and the Caribbean Development Bank.

In the context of regional economic development, further integration into the Eastern Caribbean regional economy will help enhance Grenada's competitiveness and increase its scale of economy in production, marketing and distribution.

Statistics

GDP: purchasing power parity - $360 million (2007 est.)

GDP - real growth rate: 5% (1999 est.)

GDP - per capita: purchasing power parity - $3,700 (1999 est.)

GDP - composition by sector: *agriculture:* 9.7% *industry:* 15% *services:* 75.3% (1996 est.)

Population below poverty line: NA%

Household income or consumption by percentage share: *lowest 10%:* NA% *highest 10%:* NA%

Inflation rate (consumer prices): 1.3% (1998)

Labor force: 42,300 (1996)

Labor force - by occupation: services 62%, agriculture 24%, industry 14% (1999 est.)

Unemployment rate: 15% (1997)

Budget: *revenues:* $85.8 million *expenditures:* $102.1 million, including capital expenditures of $28 million (1997)

Industries: food and beverages, textiles, light assembly operations, tourism, construction

Industrial production growth rate: 0.7% (1997 est.)

Electricity - production: 105 GWh (1998)

Electricity - production by source: *fossil fuel:* 100% *hydro:* 0% *nuclear:* 0% *other:* 0% (1998)

Electricity - consumption: 98 GWh (1998)

Electricity - exports: 0 kWh (1998)

Electricity - imports: 0 kWh (1998)

Agriculture - products: bananas, cocoa, nutmeg, mace, citrus, avocados, root crops, sugarcane, maize, vegetables

Exports: $26.8 million (1998)

Exports - commodities: bananas, cocoa, nutmeg, fruit and vegetables, clothing, mace

Exports - partners: Caricom 32.3%, United Kingdom 20%, United States 13%, Netherlands 8.8% (1991)

Imports: $200 million (1998)

Imports - commodities: food, manufactured goods, machinery, chemicals, fuel (1989)

Imports - partners: United States 31.2%, Caricom 23.6%, United Kingdom 13.8%, Japan 7.1% (1991)

Debt - external: $89.2 million (1998)

Economic aid - recipient: $8.3 million (1995)

Currency: 1 East Caribbean dollar (EC$) = 100 cents

Exchange rates: East Caribbean dollars (EC$) per US$1 - 2.7000 (fixed rate since 1976)

Fiscal year: calendar year

References

- *This article incorporates public domain material from websites or documents* [2] *of the CIA World Factbook.*

Culture of Grenada

Grenada's French colonists brought along their culture, as did the African slaves they brought across the Atlantic for agricultural work. The combination of these cultures is what you will find on this island. Indians have also influenced the island culture in more recent years.

Importantly, many descendants of the first African Grenadians have maintained their own tribal knowledge. Many Grenadians are aware of the tribe from which their ancestors came, and their dance styles have been maintained throughout the island.

With the passing of the Slave Trade Act 1807 by the British Parliament and the subsequent Abolishing of Slavery, indentured labor from India was procured at a very large scale.

The first ship, named the Maidstone, departed from Calcutta, India on January 27, 1857 and arrived a few months later on May 1. In all; 3,206 East Indians arrived to Grenada by 1885. Only 380 of them returned to India. The Indians made many contributions to Grenada. Indian Arrival Day was celebrated last year for the first time since the centenary celebration in 1957.

The Indians later on assimilated with the existing Africans, Europeans and other ethnicities intermarrying with each other. This very much influenced the culture and cuisine of Grenada.

Cuisine

Special dishes reflect the cultural diversity of Grenada. The national dish, Oil Down, is a combination of breadfruit, coconut milk, turmeric (misnamed saffron), dumplings, callaloo (taro leaves) and a salted meat such as saltfish accra (codfish), smoked herring or salt beef. It's often cooked in a large pot commonly referred to by locals as a karhee, or curry pot. Popular street foods include aloo pie, doubles and dal puri served wrapped around a curry, commonly goat, and bakes and fish cakes. Sweets include kurma, guava cheese, fudge or barfi, tamarind balls, rum and raisin ice cream and currant rolls.

Music & Festivals

Main article: Music of Grenada

Music plays a huge part in Grenadian culture with the annual Carnival competition generating new soca and calypso material in August. The rest of the time soca, calypso, and reggae are the mainstay on the minibuses competing for the loudest and, unfortunately, sometimes fastest bus service. Zouk music has also been imported to Grenada from other French Caribbean islands recently. Other local celebrations include the National Dance Festival, and Independence Day.

External links

- The Division of Culture, Grenada [1] - Official site
- Grenadian Cuisine [2]

Music of Grenada

The **music of Grenada** has included the work of several major musicians, including Eddie Bullen, David Emmanuel, one of the best-selling reggae performers ever, and Mighty Sparrow, a calypsonian. The island is also known for jazz, most notably including Kingsley Etienne, a keyboardist, while the Grenadan-American Joe Country & the Islanders have made a name in country music.

African dances brought to Grenada survive in an evolved form, as have European quadrilles and picquets. Some of the most popular recent dances include Heel-and-Toe and Carriacou Big Drum, with popular dancers including Willie Redhead, Thelma Phillips, Renalph Gebon and the Beewee Ballet.

Independence in 1974 launched a Grenadian national identity which was exemplified in the calypso of the time, which tended to be intensely patriotic. More modern calypso performers have experimented, using political commentary and poetry to expand the possibilities of Grenadian calypso. Indian influences have also changed the sound of Grenadian calypso.

Carriacou

Many years of domination by the British and the French have left behind influences in Carriacou, in songs like lullabies and reels, cantique, chanteys and quadrilles.[Europeaninfluence]

Carriacou is an island north of Grenada, best-known for the Big Drum Afro-Caribbean song-style. Big Drum dates back to at least the late 18th century.[Bigdrum] Carriacou's Afro-Caribbean population is divided into nations, each of which has a distinct rhythm that identifies it; Big Drum glorifies the ancestors of these nations, which include the Manding, Chamba, Temne, Moko, Igbo, Banda, Arada, Kongo and Cromanti.[nations] The Cromanti, being the biggest nation, begins the Big Drum ceremony with a song called "Cromanti Cudjo" (or "*Beg Pardon*"); this is followed by the other nations' songs, all of which are based on short, declamatory phrases with choruses, accompanied by two *boula* drums and a single, higher-pitched *cut drum*, both of which are made from rum barrels.[cromantidrums] Big Drum music is used to honor the memory of the dead if the deceased's family is not able to have the traditional Tombstone Feast[Tombstonefeast]

The funeral music of Carriacou is a major part of the island's folk music; Carriacouan religion centers on reverence for the "Old Parents", the apocryphal founders of the island's society.[oldparents] The saraca funerary rite, practiced on Carriacou and throughout the Grenadines, involves music, storytelling and feasting; saraca songs include both European and African lyrics.[saraca] African elements, such as the call-and-response style, are often present.

References

- "Caribbean Voyage: Carriacou Calaloo" [1]. *Musical Traditions*. Retrieved September 9, 2005.
- "Tombstone - Big Drum - Saraca" [2]. *Paradise Inn*. Retrieved September 10, 2005.

Notes

1. *Musical Traditions*
2. *Musical Traditions*
3. *Musical Traditions*
4. *Musical Traditions*
5. Paradise Inn
6. Paradise Inn
7. Paradise Inn

Further reading

- McDaniels, Lorna (1998). *The Big Drum Ritual of Carriacou: Praisesongs for Rememory of Flight*. University Press of Florida. ISBN 0-8130-1607-X.

List of birds of Grenada

This is a **list of the bird species recorded in Grenada**. The avifauna of Grenada includes a total of 168 species, of which 3 are endemic, 1 have been introduced by humans, and 97 are rare or accidental. 1 species listed is extirpated in Grenada and is not included in the species count. 3 species are globally threatened.

This list's taxonomic treatment (designation and sequence of orders, families, and species) and nomenclature (common and scientific names) follow the conventions of Clements's 5th edition. The family accounts at the beginning of each heading reflects this taxonomy, as do the species counts found in each family account. Introduced and accidental species are included in the total counts for Grenada.

The following tags have been used to highlight certain relevant categories. The commonly occurring, native, species do not fall into any of these categories.

- (A) **Accidental** A species that rarely or accidentally occurs in Grenada.
- (E) **Endemic** A species endemic to Grenada.
- (I) **Introduced** A species introduced to Grenada as a consequence, direct or indirect, of human actions.
- (Ex) **Extirpated** A species that no longer occurs in Grenada although populations exist elsewhere.

Table of contents
Non-passerines: Grebes . Shearwaters and Petrels . Storm-Petrels . Tropicbirds . Pelicans . Boobies and Gannets . Darters . Frigatebirds . Bitterns, Herons and Egrets . Storks . Ibises and Spoonbills . Ducks, Geese and Swans . New World vultures . Osprey . Hawks, Kites and Eagles . Caracaras and Falcons . Guans, Chachalacas and allies . Rails, Crakes, Gallinules, and Coots . Avocets and Stilts . Plovers and Lapwings . Sandpipers and allies . Skuas and Jaegers . Gulls . Terns . Skimmers . Pigeons and Doves . Cuckoos and Anis . Barn owls . Swifts . Hummingbirds . Kingfishers .
Passerines: Tyrant flycatchers . Swallows and Martins . Wrens . Mockingbirds and Thrashers . Thrushes and allies . Vireos . New World warblers . Bananaquit . Tanagers . Buntings, Sparrows, Seedeaters and allies . Saltators, Cardinals and allies . Troupials and allies .
See also **References**

Grebes

Order: Podicipediformes **Family**: Podicipedidae

Grebes are small to medium-large sized freshwater diving birds. They have lobed toes, and are excellent swimmers and divers. However, they have their feet placed far back on the body, making them quite ungainly on land. There are 20 species worldwide and 1 species which occur in Grenada.

- Pied-billed Grebe *Podilymbus podiceps* (A)

Shearwaters and petrels

Order: Procellariiformes **Family**: Procellariidae

The procellariids are the main group of medium-sized 'true petrels', characterised by united nostrils with a medium septum, and a long outer functional primary. There are 75 species worldwide and 1 species which occur in Grenada.

- Audubon's Shearwater *Puffinus lherminieri* (A)

Storm-Petrels

Order: Procellariiformes **Family**: Hydrobatidae

The storm-petrels are relatives of the petrels, and are the smallest of sea-birds. They feed on planktonic crustaceans and small fish picked from the surface, typically while hovering. The flight is fluttering and sometimes bat-like. There are 21 species worldwide and 1 species which occur in Grenada.

- Wilson's Storm-Petrel *Oceanites oceanicus* (A)

Tropicbirds

Order: Pelecaniformes **Family**: Phaethontidae

Tropicbirds are slender white birds of tropical oceans, with exceptionally long central tail feathers. Their heads and long wings have black markings. There are 3 species worldwide and 2 species which occur in Grenada.

- Red-billed Tropicbird *Phaethon aethereus* (A)
- White-tailed Tropicbird *Phaethon lepturus* (A)

Pelicans

Order: Pelecaniformes **Family**: Pelecanidae

Pelicans are large water birds with a distinctive pouch under the beak. As with other members of the order Pelecaniformes, they have webbed feet with four toes. There are 8 species worldwide and 1 species which occur in Grenada.

- Brown Pelican *Pelecanus occidentalis* (A)

Boobies and gannets

Order: Pelecaniformes **Family**: Sulidae

The sulids comprise the gannets and boobies. Both groups comprise medium-to-large coastal sea-birds that plunge-dive for fish. There are 9 species worldwide and 3 species which occur in Grenada.

- Masked Booby *Sula dactylatra* (A)
- Red-footed Booby *Sula sula* (A)
- Brown Booby *Sula leucogaster*

Darters

Order: Pelecaniformes **Family**: Anhingidae

Darters are frequently referred to as "snake-birds" because of their long thin neck, which gives a snake-like appearance when they swim with their bodies submerged. The males have black and dark brown plumage, an erectile crest on the nape and a larger bill than the female. The females have a much paler plumage especially on the neck and underparts. The darters have completely webbed feet, and their legs are short and set far back on the body. Their plumage is somewhat permeable, like that of cormorants, and they spread their wings to dry after diving. There are 4 species worldwide and 1 species which occur in Grenada.

- Anhinga *Anhinga anhinga* (A)

Frigatebirds

Order: Pelecaniformes **Family**: Fregatidae

Frigatebirds are large sea-birds usually found over tropical oceans. They are large, black and white or completely black, with long wings and deeply-forked tails. The males have inflatable coloured throat pouches. They do not swim or walk, and cannot take off from a flat surface. Having the largest wingspan to body weight ratio of any bird, they are essentially aerial, able to stay aloft for more than a week. There are 5 species worldwide and 1 species which occur in Grenada.

- Magnificent Frigatebird *Fregata magnificens*

Bitterns, herons and egrets

Order: Ciconiiformes **Family**: Ardeidae

The family Ardeidae contains the bitterns, herons and egrets. Herons and egrets are medium to large sized wading birds with long necks and legs. Bitterns tend to be shorter necked and more wary. Unlike other long-necked birds suck as storks, ibises and spoonbills, members of Ardeidae fly with their necks retracted. There are 61 species worldwide and 9 species which occur in Grenada.

- Great Blue Heron *Ardea herodias* (A)
- Great Egret *Ardea alba*
- Tricolored Heron *Egretta tricolor* (A)
- Little Blue Heron *Egretta caerulea* (A)
- Snowy Egret *Egretta thula* (A)
- Cattle Egret *Bubulcus ibis*
- Green Heron *Butorides virescens*
- Black-crowned Night-Heron *Nycticorax nycticorax* (A)
- Yellow-crowned Night-Heron *Nyctanassa violacea* (A)

Storks

Order: Ciconiiformes **Family**: Ciconiidae

Storks are large, long-legged, long-necked, wading birds with long, stout bills. Storks are mute; bill-clattering is an important mode of stork communication at the nest. Their nests can be large and may be reused for many years. Many species are migratory. There are 19 species worldwide and 1 species which occur in Grenada.

- Jabiru *Jabiru mycteria*

Ibises and spoonbills

Order: Ciconiiformes **Family**: Threskiornithidae

The Threskiornithidae is a family of large terrestrial and wading birds which includes the ibises and spoonbills. They have long, broad wings with 11 primary and about 20 secondary feathers. They are strong fliers and despite their size and weight, very capable soarers. There are 36 species worldwide and 3 species which occur in Grenada.

- Scarlet Ibis *Eudocimus ruber* (A)
- Glossy Ibis *Plegadis falcinellus*
- Roseate Spoonbill *Platalea ajaja*

Ducks, geese and swans

Order: Anseriformes **Family**: Anatidae

The family Anatidae includes the ducks and most duck-like waterfowl, such as geese and swans. These are birds that are modified for an aquatic existence with webbed feet, flattened bills and feathers that are excellent at shedding water due to an oily coating. There are 131 species worldwide and 12 species which occur in Grenada.

- Fulvous Whistling-Duck *Dendrocygna bicolor* (A)
- West Indian Whistling-Duck *Dendrocygna arborea* (A)
- Black-bellied Whistling-Duck *Dendrocygna autumnalis* (A)
- American Wigeon *Anas americana*
- Green-winged Teal *Anas carolinensis*
- Northern Pintail *Anas acuta*
- Blue-winged Teal *Anas discors* (A)
- Northern Shoveler *Anas clypeata*
- Ring-necked Duck *Aythya collaris*
- Lesser Scaup *Aythya affinis*
- Masked Duck *Nomonyx dominica*
- Ruddy Duck *Oxyura jamaicensis* (A)

New World vultures

Order: Falconiformes **Family**: Cathartidae

The New World vultures are not closely related to Old World vultures, but superficially resemble them because of convergent evolution. Like the Old World vultures, they are scavengers. However, unlike Old World vultures, which find carcasses by sight, New World vultures have a good sense of smell with which they locate carrion. There are 7 species worldwide, all of which are found only in the

Americas, and 1 species which occur in Grenada.

- Black Vulture *Coragyps atratus* (A)

Osprey

Order: Falconiformes **Family**: Pandionidae

The Pandionidae family contains only one species, the Osprey. The Osprey is a medium large raptor which is a specialist fish-eater with a worldwide distribution.

- Osprey *Pandion haliaetus* (A)

Hawks, kites and eagles

Order: Falconiformes **Family**: Accipitridae

Accipitridae is a family of birds of prey and include hawks, eagles, kites, harriers and Old World vultures. These birds have powerful hooked beaks for tearing flesh from their prey, strong legs, powerful talons, and keen eyesight. There are 233 species worldwide and 4 species which occur in Grenada.

- Hook-billed Kite *Chondrohierax uncinatus*
- Northern Harrier *Circus cyaneus*
- Common Black-Hawk *Buteogallus anthracinus* (A)
- Broad-winged Hawk *Buteo platypterus* (A)

Caracaras and falcons

Order: Falconiformes **Family**: Falconidae

Falconidae is a family of diurnal birds of prey. They differ from hawks, eagles, and kites in that they kill with their beaks instead of their feet. There are 62 species worldwide and 3 species which occur in Grenada.

- American Kestrel *Falco sparverius* (A)
- Merlin *Falco columbarius* (A)
- Peregrine Falcon *Falco peregrinus*

Guans, Chachalacas and allies

Order: Galliformes **Family**: Cracidae

The Cracidae are large birds, similar in general appearance to turkeys. The guans and curassows live in trees, but the smaller chachalacas are found in more open scrubby habitats. They are generally dull-plumaged, but the curassows and some guans have colourful facial ornaments. There are 50 species worldwide and 1 species which occur in Grenada.

- Rufous-vented Chachalaca *Ortalis ruficauda*

Rails, crakes, gallinules, and coots

Order: Gruiformes **Family**: Rallidae

Rallidae is a large family of small to medium-sized birds which includes the rails, crakes, coots, and gallinules. Typically they inhabit dense vegetation in damp environments near lakes, swamps, or rivers. In general they are shy and secretive birds, difficult to observe. Most species have strong legs, and have long toes which are well adapted to soft, uneven surfaces. They tend to have short, rounded wings and be weak fliers. There are 143 species worldwide and 5 species which occur in Grenada.

- Sora *Porzana carolina* (A)
- Purple Gallinule *Porphyrio martinica*
- Common Moorhen *Gallinula chloropus* (A)
- American Coot *Fulica americana* (A)
- Caribbean Coot *Fulica caribaea* (A)

Avocets and stilts

Order: Charadriiformes **Family**: Recurvirostridae

Recurvirostridae is a family of large wading birds, which includes the avocets and the stilts. The avocets have long legs and long up-curved bills. The stilts have extremely long legs and long, thin, straight bills. There are 9 species worldwide and 1 species which occur in Grenada.

- Black-necked Stilt *Himantopus mexicanus* (A)

Plovers and lapwings

Order: Charadriiformes **Family**: Charadriidae

The family Charadriidae includes the plovers, dotterels, and lapwings. They are small to medium-sized birds with compact bodies, short, thick necks and long, usually pointed, wings. They are found in open country worldwide, mostly in habitats near water, although there are some exceptions. There are 66 species worldwide and 6 species which occur in Grenada.

- American Golden-Plover *Pluvialis dominica* (A)
- Black-bellied Plover *Pluvialis squatarola* (A)
- Semipalmated Plover *Charadrius semipalmatus* (A)
- Wilson's Plover *Charadrius wilsonia* (A)
- Killdeer *Charadrius vociferus* (A)
- Collared Plover *Charadrius collaris* (A)

Sandpipers and allies

Order: Charadriiformes **Family**: Scolopacidae

The Scolopacidae are a large diverse family of small to medium sized shorebirds including the sandpipers, curlews, godwits, shanks, tattlers, woodcocks, snipes, dowitchers and phalaropes. The majority of species eat small invertebrates picked out of the mud or soil. Variation in length of legs and bills enable different species to feed in the same habitat, particularly on the coast, without direct competition for food. There are 89 species worldwide and 23 species which occur in Grenada.

- Wilson's Snipe *Gallinago delicata* (A)
- Short-billed Dowitcher *Limnodromus griseus* (A)
- Marbled Godwit *Limosa fedoa* (A)
- Eskimo Curlew *Numenius borealis* (A)
- Whimbrel *Numenius phaeopus*
- Upland Sandpiper *Bartramia longicauda* (A)
- Greater Yellowlegs *Tringa melanoleuca* (A)
- Lesser Yellowlegs *Tringa flavipes* (A)
- Solitary Sandpiper *Tringa solitaria* (A)
- Spotted Sandpiper *Actitis macularia* (A)
- Willet *Catoptrophorus semipalmatus* (A)
- Ruddy Turnstone *Arenaria interpres* (A)
- Red Knot *Calidris canutus* (A)
- Sanderling *Calidris alba* (A)
- Semipalmated Sandpiper *Calidris pusilla* (A)
- Western Sandpiper *Calidris mauri* (A)
- Least Sandpiper *Calidris minutilla* (A)
- Pectoral Sandpiper *Calidris melanotos* (A)
- Curlew Sandpiper *Calidris ferruginea* (A)
- Stilt Sandpiper *Calidris himantopus* (A)
- Buff-breasted Sandpiper *Tryngites subruficollis* (A)
- Ruff *Philomachus pugnax* (A)
- Wilson's Phalarope *Phalaropus tricolor* (A)

Skuas and jaegers

Order: Charadriiformes **Family**: Stercorariidae

The family Stercorariidae are, in general, medium to large birds, typically with grey or brown plumage, often with white markings on the wings. They nest on the ground in temperate and arctic regions and are long-distance migrants. There are 7 species worldwide and 1 species which occur in Grenada.

- Parasitic Jaeger *Stercorarius parasiticus* (A)

Gulls

Order: Charadriiformes **Family**: Laridae

Laridae is a family of medium to large birds seabirds and includes gulls and kittiwakes. They are typically grey or white, often with black markings on the head or wings. They have stout, longish bills and webbed feet. There are 55 species worldwide and 3 species which occur in Grenada.

- American Herring Gull *Larus smithsonianus*
- Black-headed Gull *Larus ridibundus* (A)
- Laughing Gull *Larus atricilla*

Terns

Order: Charadriiformes **Family**: Sternidae

Terns are a group of generally general medium to large sea-birds typically with grey or white plumage, often with black markings on the head. Most terns hunt fish by diving but some pick insects off the surface of fresh water. Terns are generally long-lived birds, with several species now known to live in excess of 25 to 30 years. There are 44 species worldwide and 9 species which occur in Grenada.

- Sandwich Tern *Sterna sandvicensis* (A)
- Royal Tern *Sterna maxima*
- Roseate Tern *Sterna dougallii* (A)
- Common Tern *Sterna hirundo* (A)
- Least Tern *Sterna antillarum* (A)
- Bridled Tern *Sterna anaethetus* (A)
- Sooty Tern *Sterna fuscata* (A)
- Black Tern *Chlidonias niger* (A)
- Brown Noddy *Anous stolidus*

Skimmers

Order: Charadriiformes **Family**: Rynchopidae

Skimmers are a small family of tropical tern-like birds. They have an elongated lower mandible which they use to feed by flying low over the water surface and skimming the water for small fish. There are 3 species worldwide and 1 species which occur in Grenada.

- Black Skimmer *Rynchops niger* (A)

Pigeons and doves

Order: Columbiformes **Family**: Columbidae

Pigeons and doves are stout-bodied birds with short necks and short slender bills with a fleshy cere. There are 308 species worldwide and 7 species which occur in Grenada.

- Rock Pigeon *Columba livia* (I)
- Scaly-naped Pigeon *Patagioenas squamosa*
- Eared Dove *Zenaida auriculata*
- Zenaida Dove *Zenaida aurita*
- Common Ground-Dove *Columbina passerina*
- Grenada Dove *Leptotila wellsi* (E)
- Ruddy Quail-Dove *Geotrygon montana*

Cuckoos and anis

Order: Cuculiformes **Family**: Cuculidae

The family Cuculidae includes cuckoos, roadrunners and anis. These birds are of variable size with slender bodies, long tails and strong legs. Unlike the cuckoo species of the Old World, North American cuckoos are not brood parasites. There are 138 species worldwide and 3 species which occur in Grenada.

- Mangrove Cuckoo *Coccyzus minor*
- Dark-billed Cuckoo *Coccyzus melacoryphus* (A)
- Smooth-billed Ani *Crotophaga ani*

Barn owls

Order: Strigiformes **Family**: Tytonidae

Barn owls are medium to large sized owls with large heads and characteristic heart-shaped faces. They have long strong legs with powerful talons. There are 16 species worldwide and 1 species which occur in Grenada.

- Barn Owl *Tyto alba*

Swifts

Order: Apodiformes **Family**: Apodidae

Swifts are small aerial birds, spending the majority of their lives flying. These birds have very short legs and never settle voluntarily on the ground, perching instead only on vertical surfaces. Many swifts have long swept-back wings that resemble a crescent or a boomerang. There are 98 species worldwide and 4 species which occur in Grenada.

- Black Swift *Cypseloides niger* (A)
- White-collared Swift *Streptoprocne zonaris* (A)
- Gray-rumped Swift *Chaetura cinereiventris*
- Short-tailed Swift *Chaetura brachyura*

Hummingbirds

Order: Trochiliformes **Family**: Trochilidae

Hummingbirds are small birds capable of hovering in mid-air due to the rapid flapping of their wings. They are the only birds that can fly backwards. There are 337 species worldwide and 9 species which occur in Grenada.

- Rufous-breasted Hermit *Glaucis hirsuta*
- White-necked Jacobin *Florisuga mellivora*
- Green-throated Mango *Anthracothorax viridigula*
- Purple-throated Carib *Eulampis jugularis*
- Green-throated Carib *Eulampis holosericeus*
- Ruby-topaz Hummingbird *Chrysolampis mosquitus*
- Antillean Crested Hummingbird *Orthorhyncus cristatus*
- White-chested Emerald *Agyrtria brevirostris*
- Copper-rumped Hummingbird *Saucerottia tobaci*

Kingfishers

Order: Coraciiformes **Family**: Alcedinidae

Kingfishers are medium-sized birds with large heads, long pointed bills, short legs, and stubby tails. There are 93 species worldwide and 1 species which occur in Grenada.

- Belted Kingfisher *Ceryle alcyon* (A)

Tyrant flycatchers

Order: Passeriformes **Family**: Tyrannidae

Tyrant flycatchers are passerine birds which occur throughout North and South America. They superficially resemble the Old World flycatchers, but are more robust with stronger bills. They do not have the sophisticated vocal capabilities of the songbirds. Most, but not all, have plain colouring. As the name implies, most are insectivorous. There are 429 species worldwide, all found only in the Americas and 7 species which occur in Grenada.

- Caribbean Elaenia *Elaenia martinica*
- Yellow-bellied Elaenia *Elaenia flavogaster*
- Euler's Flycatcher *Lathrotriccus euleri* (Ex)
- Grenada Flycatcher *Myiarchus nugator* (E)
- Tropical Kingbird *Tyrannus melancholicus* (A)
- Gray Kingbird *Tyrannus dominicensis*
- Fork-tailed Flycatcher *Tyrannus savana* (A)

Swallows and martins

Order: Passeriformes **Family**: Hirundinidae

The Hirundinidae family is a group of passerines characterized by their adaptation to aerial feeding. Their adaptations include a slender streamlined body, long pointed wings and short bills with wide gape. The feet are designed for perching rather than walking, and the front toes are partially joined at the base. There are 75 species worldwide and 4 species which occur in Grenada.

- Caribbean Martin *Progne dominicensis*
- White-winged Swallow *Tachycineta albiventer* (A)
- Bank Swallow *Riparia riparia* (A)
- Barn Swallow *Hirundo rustica*

Wrens

Order: Passeriformes **Family**: Troglodytidae

The wrens are mainly small and inconspicuous except for their loud songs. These birds have short wings and a thin down-turned bill. Several species often hold their tails upright. All are insectivorous. There are 80 species worldwide (of which all but one are New World species) and 1 species which occur in Grenada.

- House Wren *Troglodytes aedon*

Mockingbirds and Thrashers

Order: Passeriformes **Family**: Mimidae

The mimids are a family of passerine birds that includes thrashers, mockingbirds, tremblers, and the New World catbirds. These birds are notable for their vocalizations, especially their ability to mimic a wide variety of birds and other sounds heard outdoors. Their colouring tends towards dull greys and browns . There are 35 species worldwide and 4 species which occur in Grenada.

- Tropical Mockingbird *Mimus gilvus*
- Brown Trembler *Cinclocerthia ruficauda* (A)
- Scaly-breasted Thrasher *Allenia fusca* (A)
- Pearly-eyed Thrasher *Margarops fuscatus*

Thrushes and allies

Order: Passeriformes **Family**: Turdidae

The thrushes are a group of passerine birds that occur mainly in the Old World. They are plump, soft plumaged, small to medium-sized insectivores or sometimes omnivores, often feeding on the ground. Many have attractive songs. There are 335 species worldwide and 3 species which occur in Grenada.

- Gray-cheeked Thrush *Catharus minimus*
- Cocoa Thrush *Turdus fumigatus*
- Bare-eyed Thrush *Turdus nudigenis*

Vireos

Order: Passeriformes **Family**: Vireonidae

The vireos are a group of small to medium sized passerine birds restricted to the New World. They are typically greenish in colour and resemble wood warblers apart from their heavier bills. There are 52 species worldwide and 2 species which occur in Grenada.

- Yellow-throated Vireo *Vireo flavifrons* (A)

- Black-whiskered Vireo *Vireo altiloquus*

New World warblers

Order: Passeriformes **Family**: Parulidae

The New World warblers are a group of small, often colourful, passerine birds restricted to the New World. Most are arboreal, but some are terrestrial. Most members of this family are insectivores. There are 119 species worldwide and 11 species which occur in Grenada.

- Northern Parula *Parula americana* (A)
- Yellow Warbler *Dendroica petechia*
- Cape May Warbler *Dendroica tigrina* (A)
- Blackburnian Warbler *Dendroica fusca* (A)
- Prairie Warbler *Dendroica discolor* (A)
- Blackpoll Warbler *Dendroica striata* (A)
- Black-and-white Warbler *Mniotilta varia*
- American Redstart *Setophaga ruticilla* (A)
- Prothonotary Warbler *Protonotaria citrea* (A)
- Northern Waterthrush *Seiurus noveboracensis* (A)
- Louisiana Waterthrush *Seiurus motacilla*

Bananaquit

Order: Passeriformes **Family**: Coerebidae

The Bananaquit is a small passerine bird. It has a slender, curved bill, adapted to taking nectar from flowers and is the only member of the genus *Coereba* (Vieillot, 1809) and is normally placed within the family Coerebidae, although there is uncertainty whether that placement is correct.

- Bananaquit *Coereba flaveola*

Tanagers

Order: Passeriformes **Family**: Thraupidae

The tanagers are a large group of small to medium-sized passerine birds restricted to the New World, mainly in the tropics. Many species are brightly coloured. They are seed eaters, but their preference tends towards fruit and nectar. Most have short, rounded wings. There are 256 species worldwide and 4 species which occur in Grenada.

- Scarlet Tanager *Piranga olivacea* (A)
- Summer Tanager *Piranga rubra* (A)
- Antillean Euphonia *Euphonia musica* (A)

- Lesser Antillean Tanager *Tangara cucullata* (E)

Buntings, sparrows, seedeaters and allies

Order: Passeriformes **Family**: Emberizidae

The emberizids are a large family of passerine birds. They are seed-eating birds with a distinctively shaped bill. In Europe, most species are named as buntings. In North America, most of the species in this family are known as Sparrows, but these birds are not closely related to the Old World sparrows which are in the family Passeridae. Many emberizid species have distinctive head patterns. There are species 275 worldwide and 5 species which occur in Grenada.

- Blue-black Grassquit *Volatinia jacarina*
- Yellow-bellied Seedeater *Sporophila nigricollis* (A)
- Black-faced Grassquit *Tiaris bicolor*
- Lesser Antillean Bullfinch *Loxigilla noctis*
- Grassland Yellow-Finch *Sicalis luteola* (A)

Saltators, Cardinals and allies

Order: Passeriformes **Family**: Cardinalidae

The cardinals are a family of passerine birds that are robust, seed-eating birds, with strong bills. They are typically associated with open woodland. The sexes usually have distinct plumages. There are 43 species worldwide and 1 species which occur in Grenada.

- Rose-breasted Grosbeak *Pheucticus ludovicianus*

Troupials and allies

Order: Passeriformes **Family**: Icteridae

The icterids are a group of small to medium, often colourful, passerine birds restricted to the New World and include the grackles, New World blackbirds, and New World orioles. Most species have black as the predominant plumage colour, often enlivened by yellow, orange or red. There are 98 species worldwide and 5 species which occur in Grenada.

- Bobolink *Dolichonyx oryzivorus* (A)
- Carib Grackle *Quiscalus lugubris*
- Shiny Cowbird *Molothrus bonariensis*
- Venezuelan Troupial *Icterus icterus* (A)
- Baltimore Oriole *Icterus galbula* (A)

See also

- List of birds
- Lists of birds by region

References

- Lepage, Denis. "Checklist of birds of Grenada" [1]. *Bird Checklists of the World*. Avibase. Retrieved 26 April 2007.
- Clements, James F. (2000). *Birds of the World: a Checklist*. Cornell University Press. pp. 880. ISBN 0-934797-16-1.

Overview of St.George's

St. George's, Grenada

St. George's	
— City —	
St. Georges	
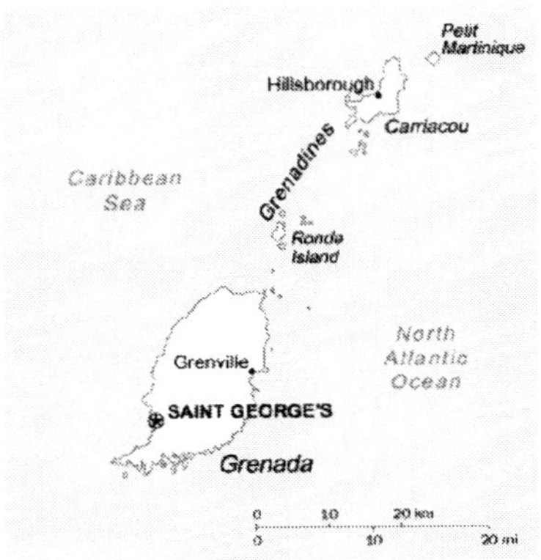 St.Georges within Grenada	
Coordinates: 12°3′N 61°45′W	
Country	Grenada
Parish	Saint George
Population (1999)	
- Total	7,500
Time zone	UTC-4

St. George's, population 7,500 (1999), with an agglomeration of 33,000 people is the capital of Grenada. The city is surrounded by a hillside of an old volcano crater and is on a horseshoe-shaped harbour.

The city is a popular Caribbean tourist destination that attracts thousands of tourists, cruise ships, and even celebrities. The city has significantly developed in recent years, while preserving its rich history, culture, and natural beauty. The city is home of St. George's University School of Medicine. The main exports are cacao, nutmeg, and mace.

History

St. George's was built by the French in 1650. This is made apparent by the many red roofed houses in the city. After the Great Fire of 1771, most of the boarding houses on Granby Street were moved to Gouyave. On the 1st of November 1775 there were a Great Fire in the town of St. George's known as the **Great Fire of St George's** .

Following the withdrawal of Bridgetown, Barbados, in the mid 1880s, St. George's went on to become the replacement capital of the former colony of the British Windward Islands.

The Tikal was the first art cater shop in Grenada and it was opened in December 1959. In 2004, St. George's and the rest of Grenada were severely battered by Hurricane Ivan. The hurricane left significant destruction across the island and crippled much of the island's infrastructure. It was estimated that some 90% of the island's homes had sustained damage and the nutmeg trees which are key to Grenada's economy were devastated. A year later with the help of international donors (Canada, the United States, and the European Union) Grenada had experienced a significant turn around in rebuilding efforts. By 2007, Grenada had participated as planned in the hosting of the 2007 Cricket World Cup.

Hospitals

- General Hospital
- Mount Gay Hospital
- Old Trafford Medical Center
- St Augustine's Medical Services
- St. George's University School of Medicine
- Marryshows' Hospital & Health Clinic
- Salus Clinic

Main sites

- Roman Catholic Cathedral built in 1818
- Anglican Church built in 1825
- Wharf Road
- Fort George built by the French in 1705
- St. Georges fresh produce marketplace
- Grande Anse beach, shopping centers, hotels
- Maurice Bishop International Airport (Point(e) Saline)
- Grenada National Museum
- Parliament Building, also known as York House, houses the House of Representatives, the Senate, and the Supreme Court
- Governor General Residence, Government Offices
- Fort Frederick Fort Complex
- Queen's Park Stadium Complex, built by the Chinese to host part of the 2007 Cricket World Cup

External links

- Images of St. George's [1]

Saint George Parish, Grenada

St. George Parish	
— Parish —	
Nickname(s): The Cathedral Parish	
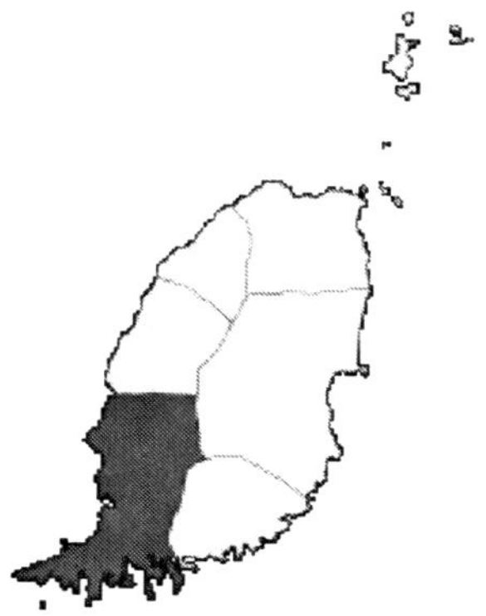	
Country	Grenada
Capital City	St. George
Area	
- Total	26 sq mi (67 km^2)
Population	
- Total	37,057
- Density	1416.7/sq mi (547/km^2)

St. George's, Grenada, 2000

Saint George is one of the parishes of Grenada, located on the south-western end of the island. The capital of Grenada, St. George's, is located in this parish, and it is regarded as the most picturesque capital in the Caribbean. Its horseshoe-shaped harbour is surrounded by the pastel colors of warehouses and it is not uncommon to see red-tiled roofs on traditional shops and homes. Saint George is also the home of the world famous Grand Anse Beach and many of the island's holiday resorts.

The peninsula at the south-western tip of Saint George is called Point Salines, and Grenada's only active airport, Maurice Bishop International Airport, is located here. The tourist infrastructure is more extensive in Saint George than in the rest of the island, due to the airport, capital city and most popular beaches all being found in this parish. It is also home to St. George's University.

As of 2001, Saint George has a population of 35,559, making it the most populous parish of Grenada. It is also the second largest, with an area of 26 sq mi.

References

Geographical coordinates: 12°3′N 61°45′W

Cities Nearby to See

Parishes of Grenada

Grenada Parishes	
Category	Parish
Location	Grenada
Number	6

Grenada

This article is part of the series:
Politics and government of Grenada

- Queen
  - Elizabeth II
- Governor-General
  - Carlyle Glean
- Prime Minister
  - Tillman Thomas
- Parliament
  - Senate
  - House of Representatives
- Political parties
- Elections: 2003, 2008
- Parishes
- Foreign relations

Other countries · Atlas
Politics portal

The Caribbean island country of Grenada is subdivided into sub-regions known as parishes.

A parish defines a territorial unit or region that, historically, was usually an area under the pastoral care served by a local church as an ecclesiastical administrative unit (see Parish) and later used by map-makers to set boundaries to an area of land. Traditionally a settlement or village would centre around a church and later grow to become a town and then even a city. Therefore a parish has now come to mean an administrative division and is used so by several countries as the smallest unit (or lowest tier) of local government.

The differing size and shape of each parish was primarily influenced by the island's earlier history and land that was granted to the first settlers that claimed that territory during the colonial years of the island.

Two decades after Barbados was settled the French governor of Martinique, Jacques-Dyel du Parquet, purchased Grenada from a French company and in 1650 established a settlement at what was to be Fort Royal in the parish of the low lands (*Ville Ft. Royal situé à Paroisse de la Basse Terre*). During this time the parish boundaries where laid out.

The French cartographer Jacques-Nicolas Bellin (1703–1772) draw several editions of a chart of the island of Grenada showing the earlier French parish divisions and was published as *Carte de L'Isle de la Grenade* in Paris 1756.
However, by 1763 the island was under British rule and a later map of the Island of Grenada showing towns and villages and division of the island into quarters in English by cartographer Bryon Edwards (for J. Cooke's *History of the West Indies*) was engraved in 1818.

After a century the French capitulated to the British and formally ceded the island to Britain in 1763 by the Treaty of Paris. The English took over the churches and, as was traditional, chaples of ease and local churches were elevated to parish church status across the island, leading to the formation of new parishes surrounding those newly named churches. The six boundaries or borders of these parishes having already been well established in the mindset of the people then living simply took on the names of these churches.

The nation's capital St. George's, which is located within the parish of Saint George, and even to this day the original parishional border-lines are still well defined.

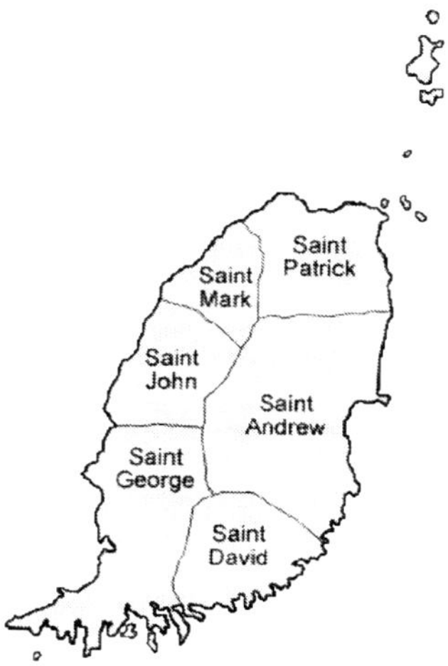

The eleven parishes are:

Nr.	*Parish*	Former Capitals	Land Area (km²)	Population (census 2001)	Density km^{-2}
1	Saint Andrew	Grenville	99	24,749	249.98
2	Saint David	St. David's	44	11,486	261.04
3	Saint George	St. George's	65	37,057	570.10
4	Saint John	Gouyave	35	8,591	245.46
5	Saint Mark	Victoria	25	3,994	159.76
6	Saint Patrick	Sauteurs	42	10,674	254.14
	These two islands are of the Grenadines, have the status of dependency.				
—	Carriacou	Hillsborough	34	6,081	178.85
—	Petite_Martinique		2.4	900	375.00
	Grenada	St. George's	344	102,632	298.35

See also

- ISO 3166-2:GD

Saint Andrew Parish, Grenada

Saint Andrew's Parish

— Parish —

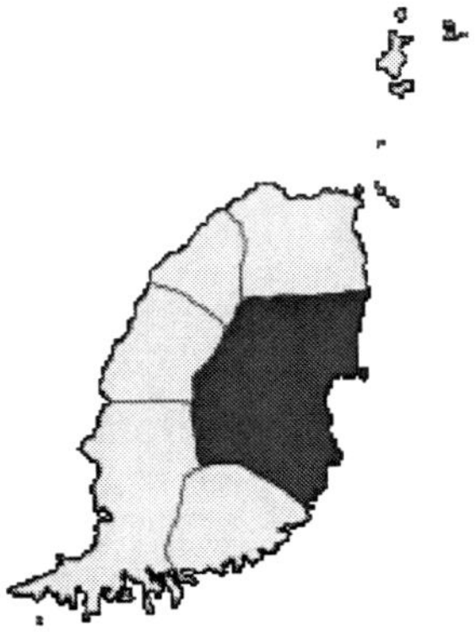

Country	Grenada
Capital City	Grenville
Area	
- Total	35 sq mi (91 km^2)
Population	
- Total	24,749
- Density	644.9/sq mi (249/km^2)

Saint Andrew's is the largest parish in Grenada. The main town is Grenville, which is also Grenada's second largest town after St George's. Grenville is also known as La Baye (its former French name).

History

In 1650's the French named the parish **Morne de Combat** and it was part of the French Territories. Marquis was the first Parish Capital from 1795 to 1796, Grenville became capital of Saint Andrew's in 1796.

Geographical coordinates: 12°07′09″N 61°37′35″W

Saint John Parish, Grenada

Saint John Parish

— Parish —

St. Georges

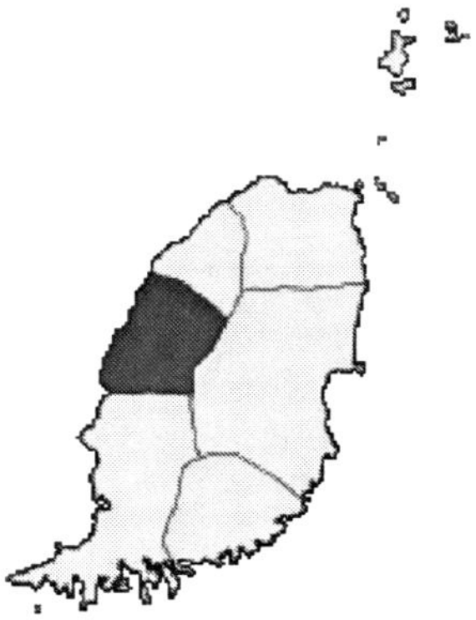

Country	Grenada
Capital City	Gouyave
Area	
- Total	15 sq mi (39 km^2)
Population	
- Total	8,591
- Density	632/sq mi (244/km^2)

Saint John is one of the parishes of Grenada. Its capital is Gouyave. It is known locally as the action city and the place that never sleeps. Fishing is the main industry. Gouyave is also the home of

Grenada's biggest nutmeg factory and of the Dougladston Estate and old Spice Plantation. There is almost no tourism in this parish of Grenada, with only a few small guesthouses such as the Mango Bay Cottages [1] in Woodford.

History

In 1889, an iron bridge was built on a new boulder bank between Gouyave and the neighbourhood of Florida. On Nov. 8, 1897, there were heavy rains in the parish, which nearly flooded the Gouyave River. On Dec. 6, 1897 the Gouyave-Florida boulder bank and stone bridge were destroyed. Gouyave was alson known as Charlotte town.

Constituency

Saint John Constituency	
— Constituency —	
Country	Grenada
Parish	St John
Constituency Minister	Michael Church
Capital City	Gouyave

Year	Winner	Party
1984–1990	Grace M. Duncan	Grenada National Party
1990–1995	Edzel V. Thomas	Grenada United Labour Party
1995–1999	Grace M. Duncan	New National Party
1999–2008	Claris C. T. Charles	New National Party
2008-Date	Michael A. Church	National Democratic Congress

External links

- www.gogouyave.com [2]
- www.gouyavefishfriday.com [3]
- www.mangobaygrenada.com [2]

Geographical coordinates: 12°10′N 61°44′W

Saint Patrick Parish, Grenada

Saint Patrick Parish	
— Parish —	
St Patrick parish sign	
Nickname(s): The Agriculture Parish The Historical Parish	

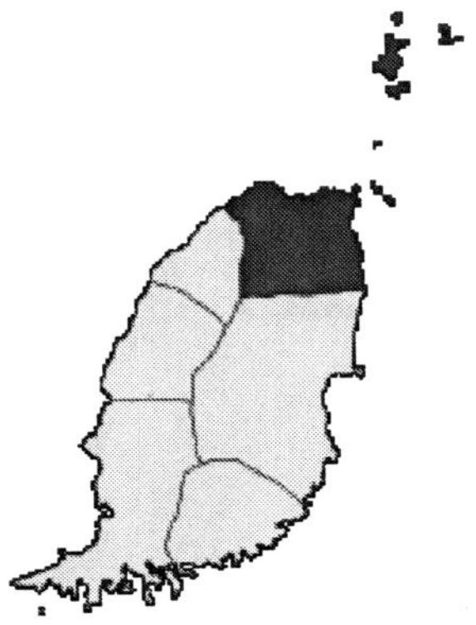

Country	Grenada
Capital City	Sauteurs
Area	
- Total	17 sq mi (44 km^2)
Population	
- Total	10,674
- Density	655.3/sq mi (253/km^2)

Saint Patrick is one of the parishes of Grenada, covering the north of the country. A spectacular coastline with several fine bays faces several small islands to the north. Its most famous beach is Bathway. The principal town in St. Patrick is Sauteurs. One of the most famous landmarks in the town is the Leapers' Hill, where legend has it that the indigenous Caribs jumped over the cliff and into the sea to escape colonization by the French.

Several volcanic cones and craters are located within the parish, such as the Punchbowl and Lake Antoine.

For much of the last century, the parish was heavily agricultural with several large estates accounting for a significant share of cocoa and nutmeg production in Grenada.

History

In the 18th and the 19th Centuries Irvin's Bay was a working harbour for shipping sugar and other produce grown from nearby estates and the Bay House were shipped to England and France. On Wednesday, 1 May 1867, the Maidstone sailing ship wereWikipedia:Please clarify carrying 289 Calcutta Indians to Irvin's Bay for labour shortage on Grenada estates.

References

• "St. Catherine - Synonyms & Subfeatures" [1]. Global Volcanism Program, Smithsonian Institution.

Geographical coordinates: 12°12′11″N 61°38′26″W

Amber Belair

Amber Belair	
— Community —	

Location within Grenada

Coordinates: 12°00′14″N 61°45′43″W	
Country	Grenada
Parish	Saint George
Time zone	UTC-4

Amber Belair is a community in Saint George Parish, Grenada. It is located at the southern end of the island.

Bacolet, Grenada

Bacolet	
— Village —	

Bacolet

Location within Grenada

Coordinates: 12°2′N 61°41′W	
Country	Grenada
Parish	Saint David
Elevation	125 ft (38 m)
Time zone	UTC-4

Bacolet, Grenada is a town in the south-east of Grenada, Caribbean. It is also referred to as *Baillies Bacolet*.

External links

- Map with Bacelot, Grenada [1]

Barique

Barique	
— Village —	

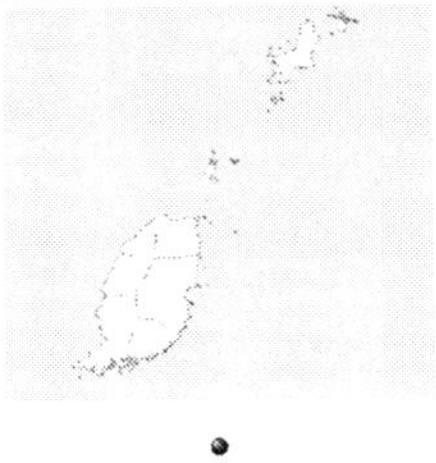

Barique

Location within Grenada

Coordinates: 12°10′N 61°39′W	
Country	Grenada
Parish	Saint Patrick
Elevation	948 ft (289 m)
Time zone	UTC-4

Barique is a town in Saint Patrick Parish, Grenada. It is located at the northern end of the island.

Becke Moui

Becke Moui	
— Village —	

Becke Moui

Location within Grenada

Coordinates: 12°01′N 61°42′W	
Country	Grenada
Parish	Saint David
Elevation	3 ft (1 m)
Time zone	UTC-4

Becke Moui is a town in Saint David Parish, Grenada. It is located at the southern end of the island, along the southern coast.

Belmont, Grenada

Belmont	
— Town —	

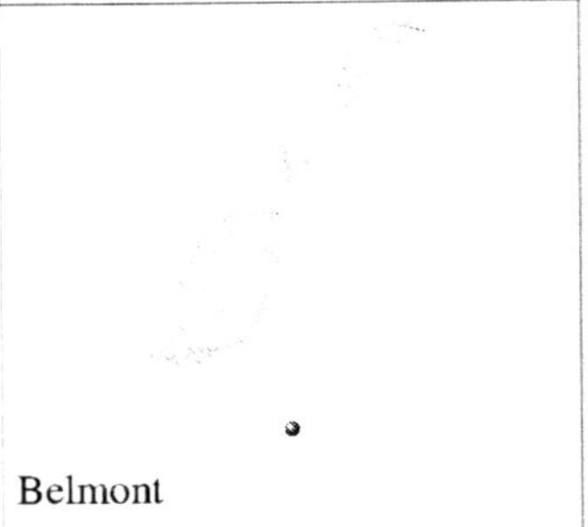

Location within Grenada

Coordinates: 12°9′59″N 61°38′1″W	
Country	Grenada
Parish	Saint Patrick
Elevation	331 ft (101 m)
Time zone	UTC-4

Belmont is a town in Saint Patrick parish in Grenada.

Bogles

Bogles

— **Town** —

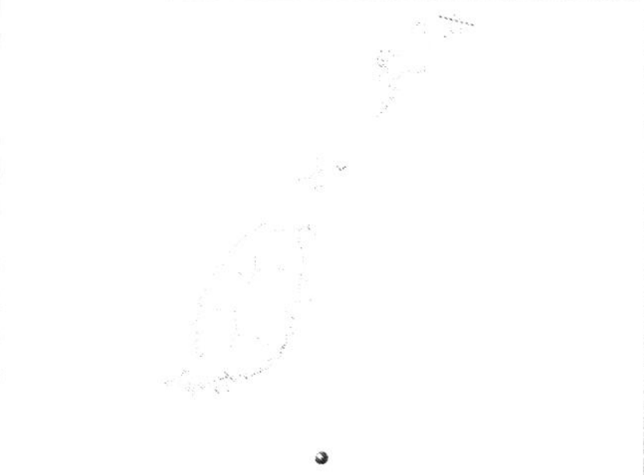

Bogles

Location within Grenada

Coordinates: 12°30′N 61°26′W

Country	Grenada
Dependency	Carriacou and Petite Martinique
Elevation	118 ft (36 m)
Time zone	UTC-4

Bogles is a town on the island of Carriacou in Grenada.

Bois de Gannes

Bois de Gannes

— Village —

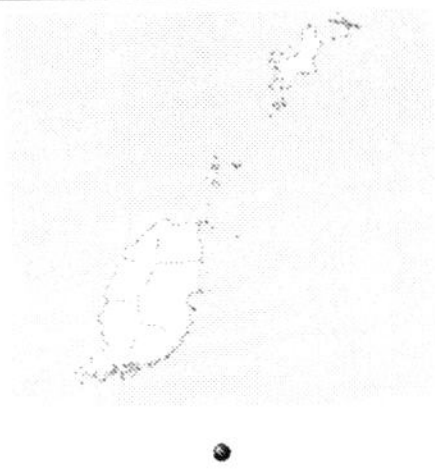

Bois de Gannes

Location within Grenada

Coordinates: 12°02′N 61°42′W

Country	Grenada
Parish	Saint David
Elevation	341 ft (104 m)
Time zone	UTC-4

Bois de Gannes is a town in Saint David Parish, Grenada. It is located towards the southern end of the island.

Deblando

Deblando	
— Village —	

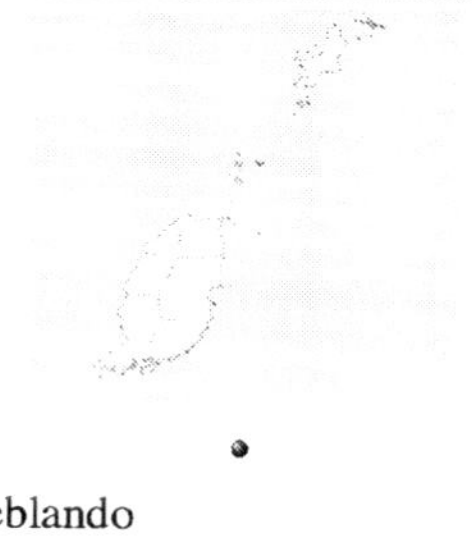

Location within Grenada

Coordinates: 12°06′N 61°38′W	
Country	Grenada
Parish	Saint Andrew
Elevation	151 ft (46 m)
Time zone	UTC-4

Deblando is a town in Saint Andrew Parish, Grenada. It is located at along the island's eastern coast.[citation needed]

Diego Piece

Diego Piece	
— Settlement —	

Location within Grenada

Coordinates: 12°12′N 61°40′W	
Country	Grenada
Elevation	866 ft (264 m)
Time zone	UTC-4

Diego Piece is a settlement in Grenada. It is located at the northern end of the island.

Elie Hall

Elie Hall	
— Village —	

Elie Hall

Location within Grenada

Coordinates: 12°12′N 61°38′W	
Country	Grenada
Parish	Saint Patrick
Elevation	253 ft (77 m)
Time zone	UTC-4

Elie Hall is a town in Saint Patrick Parish, Grenada. It is located near the northern end of the island.

Grand Roy

Grand Roy	
— Town —	
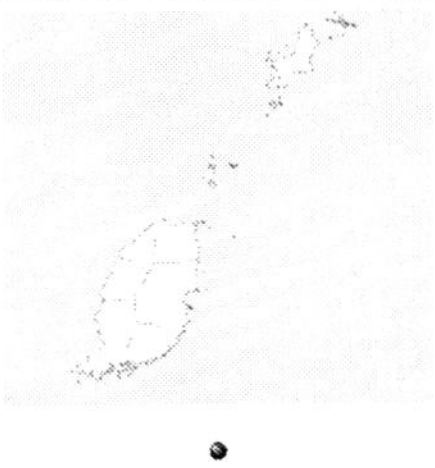 Grand Roy Location within Grenada	
Coordinates: 12°07′N 61°45′W	
Country	Grenada
Parish	Saint John
Elevation	89 ft (27 m)
Population	
- Total	2400
Time zone	UTC-4

Grand Roy is a town in Grenada. It is located on the island's west coast, to the north of Marigot on the road to Gouyave.

Ka-fe Beau

Ka-fe Beau	
— Village —	

Ka-fe Beau

Location within Grenada

Coordinates: 12°02′N 61°45′W	
Country	Grenada
Parish	Saint George
Elevation	187 ft (57 m)
Time zone	UTC-4

Ka-fe Beau is a town in Saint George Parish, Grenada. It is located at the southern end of the island, on the western coast.

L'Anse Aux Epines

L'Anse Aux Epines

— Residential community —

L'Anse Aux Epines

Location within Grenada

Coordinates: 11°59′40″N 61°45′22″W

Country	Grenada
Parish	Saint George
Time zone	UTC-4

L'Anse Aux Epines is a primarily residential community in Saint George Parish, Grenada. This peninsular forms the most southerly tip of Grenada.

Mamma Cannes

Mamma Cannes	
— Village —	

Mamma Cannes

Location within Grenada

Coordinates: 12°04′N 61°39′W	
Country	Grenada
Parish	Saint Andrew
Elevation	367 ft (112 m)
Time zone	UTC-4

Mamma Cannes is a town in Saint Andrew Parish, Grenada. It is located on the eastern coast of the island.

Marquis, Grenada

Marquis

— Town —

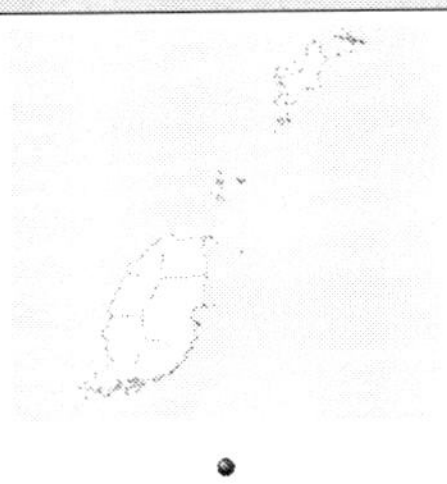

Marquis
Location within Grenada

Coordinates: 12°05′N 61°37′W

Country	Grenada
Parish	Saint Andrew
Elevation	0 ft (0 m)
Time zone	UTC-4

Marquis is a town in Grenada. It is located on the island's east coast, to the south of Grenville on the road to Pomme Rose and St. David's.

History

In 1795-1796 the hill of *Battle Hill* in Marquis was own by the French. Marquis was the first capital city of the parish of Saint Andrew's from 1795 to 1796. The Marquis Pentecostal Church is the Oldest Pentecostal Assemblies of the West Indies (PAWI) church in Grenada and it was Established on May 1927.

Maulti

Maulti	
— Village —	

Maulti

Location within Grenada

Coordinates: 12°02′N 61°40′W	
Country	Grenada
Parish	Saint David
Elevation	26 ft (8 m)
Time zone	UTC-4

Maulti is a town in Saint David Parish, Grenada. It is located along the island's southern coast.

Morne Docteur

Morne Docteur	
— Village —	

Location within Grenada

Coordinates: 12°06′N 61°45′W	
Country	Grenada
Parish	Saint George
Elevation	276 ft (84 m)
Time zone	UTC-4

Morne Docteur is a town in Saint George Parish, Grenada. It is located on the western coast of the island.

Morne Fendue

Morne Fendue	
— Village —	

Morne Fendue

Location within Grenada

Coordinates: 12°12′N 61°38′W	
Country	Grenada
Parish	Saint Patrick
Elevation	253 ft (77 m)
Time zone	UTC-4

Morne Fendue is a town in Saint Patrick Parish, Grenada. It is located at the northern end of the island.

Morne Jaloux Ridge

Morne Jaloux Ridge	
— Morne Jaloux is not a town it's a small community overlooking the other low lands communities like Springs Dixie Belmont GrandAnse woodlands and more —	
Nickname(s): Jealous Mountain	
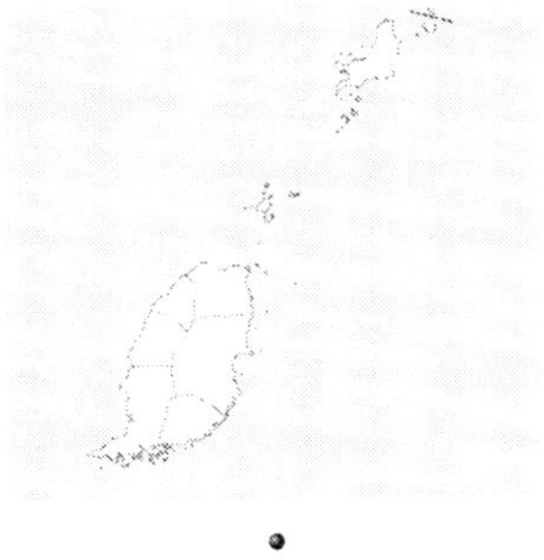 Morne Jaloux Ridge Location within Grenada	
Coordinates: 12°02′N 61°44′W	
Country	Grenada
Parish	Saint George
Elevation	423 ft (129 m)
Time zone	UTC-4

Morne Jaloux Ridge is a town in Saint George Parish, Grenada. It is located towards the southern end of the island, to the north of Morne Jaloux.

Morne Jaloux

Morne Jaloux	
— Village —	
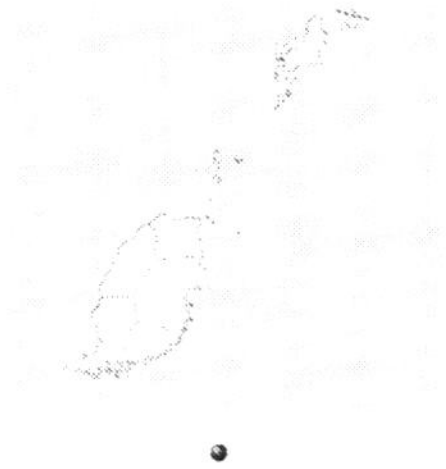 Morne Jaloux Location within Grenada	
Coordinates: 12°1′0″N 61°44′0″W	
Country	Grenada
Parish	Saint George
Elevation	210 ft (64 m)
Time zone	UTC-4

Morne Jaloux is a town in Saint George Parish, Grenada. It is located at the southern end of the island.

Morne Longue

Morne Longue	
— Village —	

Morne Longue

Location within Grenada

Coordinates: 12°07′N 61°41′W	
Country	Grenada
Parish	Saint Andrew
Time zone	UTC-4

Morne Longue is a town in Saint Andrew Parish, Grenada. It is located at the center of the island.

Morne Rouge

Morne Rouge	
— Village —	

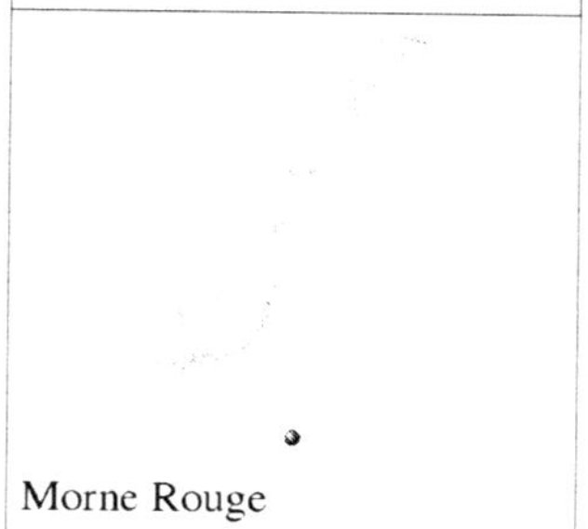

Location within Grenada

Coordinates: 12°01′N 61°46′W	
Country	Grenada
Parish	Saint George
Elevation	33 ft (10 m)
Time zone	UTC-4

Morne Rouge is a town in Saint George Parish, Grenada. It is located at the southern end of the island, near its very tip.

Morne Tranquille

Morne Tranquille	
— Village —	

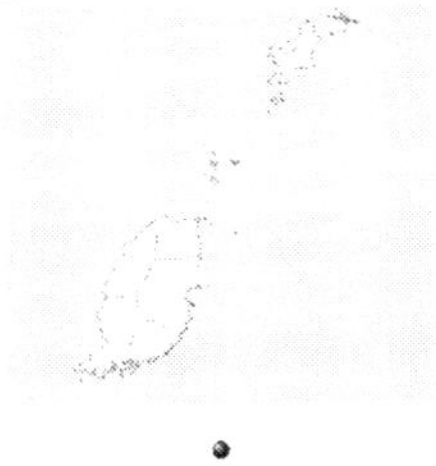

Morne Tranquille
Location within Grenada

Coordinates: 12°03′N 61°42′W	
Country	Grenada
Parish	Saint David
Elevation	463 ft (141 m)
Time zone	UTC-4

Morne Traquille is a town in Saint David Parish, Grenada. It is located somewhat inland from the southern end of the island.

Mount Craven

Mount Craven	
— Village —	

Welcome Sign

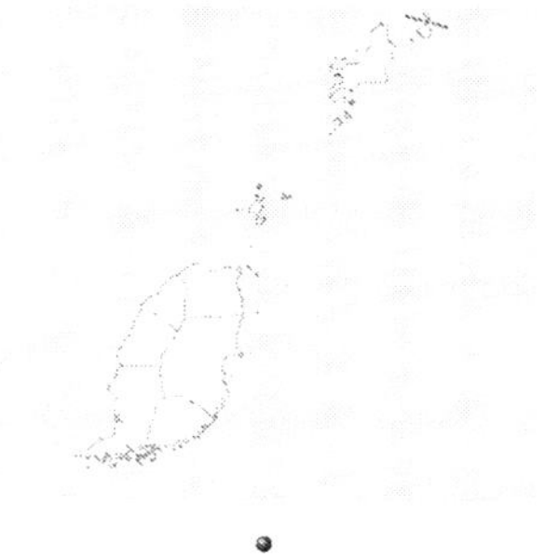
Mount Craven

Location within Grenada

Coordinates: 12°13′N 61°39′W	
Country	Grenada
Parish	Saint Patrick
Elevation	289 ft (88 m)
Time zone	UTC-4

Mount Craven is a village in Grenada. It is located on the island's north coast, near the parish capital, Sauteurs.

Paradise, Grenada

Paradise	
— Town —	

Paradise

Location within Grenada

Coordinates: 12°8′27″N 61°41′33″W	
Country	Grenada
Parish	Saint John
Elevation	663 ft (202 m)
Time zone	UTC-4

Paradise is a town in Saint John Parish, Grenada. It is located in the east of the island, between Grenville and Dunfermline.

St. David's, Grenada

St. David's	
— Village —	

St. David's

Location within Grenada

Coordinates: 12°1′58″N 61°39′59″W	
Country	Grenada
Parish	Saint David
Elevation	26 ft (8 m)
Time zone	UTC-4

St. David's is a town in Saint David Parish, Grenada. It is located between La tante and Westerhall in the island's southeast.

Tivoli, Grenada

Tivoli	
— Village —	

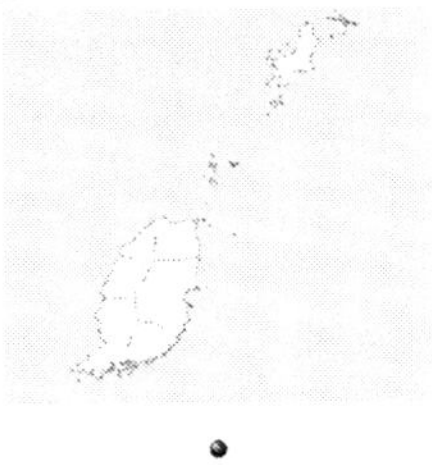

Tivoli

Location within Grenada

Coordinates: 12°10′N 61°37′W	
Country	Grenada
Parish	Saint Patrick
Elevation	23 ft (7 m)
Time zone	UTC-4

Tivoli is a town in Grenada. It is located in the northeast of the island, on the River Antoine.

Union Village, Grenada

Union Village	
— Village —	

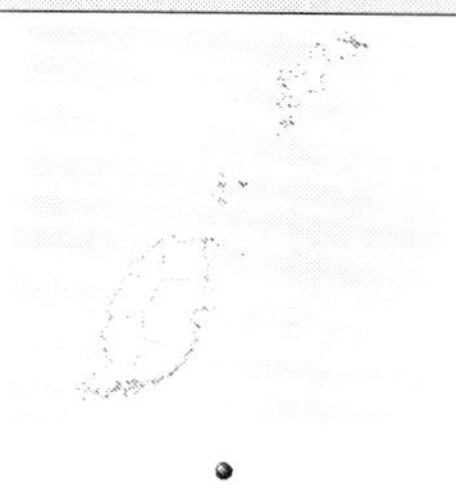

Union Village

Location within Grenada

Coordinates: 12°06′N 61°38′W	
Country	Grenada
Parish	Saint Andrew
Elevation	151 ft (46 m)
Time zone	UTC-4

Union Village is a town in Saint Andrew Parish, Grenada. It is located on the island's eastern coast.

Union, Grenada

Union

— Village —

Location within Grenada

Coordinates: 12°12′00″N 61°40′00″W

Country	Grenada
Parish	Saint Patrick
Elevation	866 ft (264 m)
Time zone	UTC-4

Union is a town in Saint Patrick Parish, Grenada. It is located towards the northern end of the island.

Upper La Tante

Upper La Tante	
— Village —	

Location within Grenada

Coordinates: 12°03′N 61°39′W	
Country	Grenada
Parish	Saint David
Elevation	108 ft (33 m)
Time zone	UTC-4

Upper La Tante is a town in Saint David Parish, Grenada. It is located towards the southern end of the island.

Upper Capitol

Upper Capitol	
— Village —	

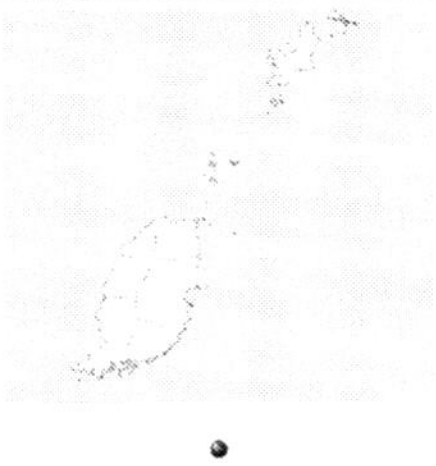

Upper Capitol
Location within Grenada

Coordinates: 12°07′N 61°40′W	
Country	Grenada
Parish	Saint Andrew
Elevation	955 ft (291 m)
Time zone	UTC-4

Upper Capitol is a town in Saint Andrew Parish, Grenada. It is located towards the northern end of the island. It is adjacent to St. James, and a part of the bigger Birch Grove community

Upper Conference

Upper Conference	
— Village —	

Upper Conference
Location within Grenada

Coordinates: 12°09′N 61°37′W	
Country	Grenada
Parish	Saint Andrew
Elevation	7 ft (2 m)
Time zone	UTC-4

Upper Conference is a town in Saint Andrew Parish, Grenada. It is located towards the northern end of the island, along the eastern coast.

Upper La Taste

Upper La Taste	
— Village —	
 Location within Grenada	
Coordinates: 12°11′N 61°37′W	
Country	Grenada
Parish	Saint Patrick
Elevation	207 ft (63 m)
Time zone	UTC-4

Upper La Taste is a town in Saint Patrick Parish, Grenada. It is located towards the northern end of the island, along the eastern coast.

Upper Pearls

Upper Pearls	
— Village —	

Upper Pearls

Location within Grenada

Coordinates: 12°09′N 61°37′W	
Country	Grenada
Parish	Saint Andrew
Elevation	7 ft (2 m)
Time zone	UTC-4

Upper Pearls is a town in Saint Andrew Parish, Grenada. It is located towards the northern end of the island, along the east coast.

Things to See in and Around the City

Hillsborough, Carriacou

Hillsborough	
— City —	
 Hillsborough	
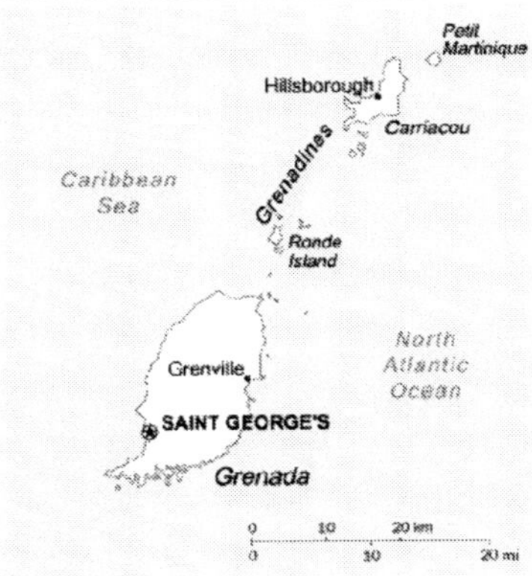 Hillsborough within Carriacou, Grenada	
Coordinates: 12°29′N 61°28′W	
Country	Grenada
Dependency	Carriacou and Petite Martinique
Elevation	20 ft (6 m)

Population (1999)	
- Total	1000
Time zone	UTC-4

Hillsborough is a small town with approx. 1,000 people living there. It is the main town on Carriacou and is its capital. It home to Carriacou Museum used to be a cotton gin mill and now the museum managed by Carriacou Historical Society. The is on Paterson Street of the centre in town.

Carriacou and Petite Martinique

Carriacou and Petite Martinique		

Anthem: *Hail Grenada* **Royal anthem:** *God Save the Queen*		
Capital (and largest city)		Hillsborough 12°48′N 61°46′W
Official language(s)		English, Patois
Demonym		Carriacouan, Petit Martiniquian
Government		Dependency of Grenada
-	Queen	Queen Elizabeth II
-	Governor General	Carlyle Glean
-	Prime Minister	Tillman Thomas
-	Member of Parliament	Elvin G Nimrod
-	Ministry of Carriacou and Petite Martinique Affairs	Senator George Prime
Establishment		
-	British Grenada control established	1763
-	Grenada control established	February 7, 1974
-	became constituency	1944
Area		
-	Total	37.7 km^2 13.2 sq mi
Population		
-	estimate	10,000
Currency		East Caribbean dollar (XCD)
Time zone		(UTC−4)
-	Summer (DST)	(UTC−4)
Drives on the		left

Internet TLD	.gd
Calling code	1 473
The main Patois language is Kweyol (French Patois).	

Carriacou Island in the Caribbean Sea, is the largest island of the Grenadines, an archipelago in the Windward Islands chain. The island is 13 sq miles (34 km²), and a dependency of Grenada with a population of 4,595 (1991 census). The main settlements on the island are Hillsborough, L'Esterre, Harvey Vale, and Windward.

View from Hillsborough looking south over the beach.

The neighbouring island of **Petite Martinique** is 2½ miles away from Carriacou, and also a part of Grenada. With its 586 acres (2.4 km²), population 900, it is smaller than Carriacou. The residents of this island live by boat-building, fishing and seafaring.

The Grenadine islands to the north of Carriacou and Petite Martinique belong to the nation of St. Vincent and the Grenadines.

Nautical Chart of Carriacou from 1891

Geography

A view of Carriacou.

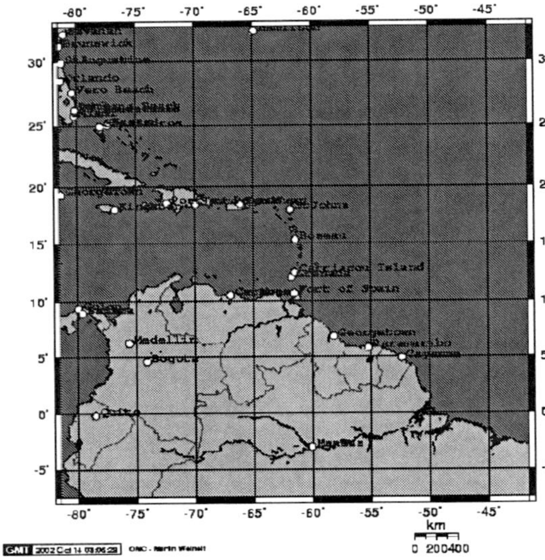

Locator Map

Carriacou is the largest of the Grenadines and is characterized by hilly terrain sloping to white sand beaches. The island stretches from Pegus Point in the south to Gun point in the north and it is about 16 miles long.

The island has several natural harbors and many coral reefs and small offshore islets.[1]

The highest point on the island is High Point North at 955 feet.[2]

Carriacou has no rivers. Residents rely on rainfall for their water. The dry season is between January and June when the Trade Winds dominate the climate.

History

Carriacou

A view of Hillsborough, Carriacou

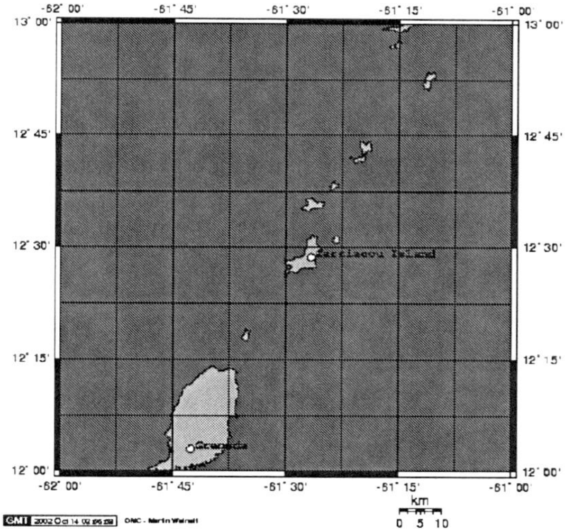

Map of Carriacou Island near Grenada

Main article: History of Carriacou

The earliest settlers, the Amerindians, called Carriacou *"Kayryouacou"*, meaning "the land of reefs."

In 1656, Père du Tertre from Guadeloupe visited Carriacou and he was the first French/European person (turtle Fisherman) to visit Carriacou. [*citation needed*]. The island of Carriacou was originally settled by the French

In 1720, Bartholomew Roberts captured a French ship near Carriacou and commandeered it, renaming it the *Royal Fortune*. In 1750, the first census of the island was conducted, and there were 199 people (92 Whites, 92 Blacks and 15 Mulattos) living in Carriacou. In 1763 was ceded with Grenada to the British when they captured neighbouring Grenada. In 1776, the island population was 3,239 (86 Whites and 3,153 slaves) people, not counting the free Blacks and the free Mulattos. In 1791, Gun Point (Rapid Point) which had been a division of the Grenadines, was made a latitude on the island, but the point belonged to Saint Vincent and the rest of Carriacou belonged to Grenada.

In 1870, Stephen Joseph Perry went in charge of a government expedition to observe a solar eclipse at Carriacou. The first record of a hurricane on the island was on August 14, 1944. Bishop's College was the first Secondary School in Carriacou, it was opened in 1964 and the Anglican Church established this school. In 1968 Lauriston airport/airstrip was opened. On October 31, 1975 Carriacou Carib Organization (CGO) began. In 1922, Petite Charles first introduced the Jab Jab (Devil) Mas to Carriacou. In the 19th century, the Pierrot Mas was first introduced to Carriacou. In 1965, the Carriacou Regatta began. The Telephone system began operating in 1961 on the island of Carriacou.

The inhabitants of Carriacou perform the *"Big Drum"* or *"Nation"* dance which celebrates their West African ancestors that were brought to the island during slavery. These Big Drum dances are usually performed at *"Maroons"* village festivals or **fetes**, where food and drink are prepared. They can also be danced at wakes and tombstone feasts in honor of dead relatives.

There still is a traditional boat-building culture located in the village of Windward, on the northeastern side of the island, where Carriacou's people of Scottish and Irish ancestry are concentrated.

Carriacouans have migrated to the United Kingdom, and especially to the county town of Bedford. It is said that if you live in Carriacou you will have a family member in Bedford, and if you live in Bedford you will surely know someone from Carriacou. Other English locations where Kayaks congregate are Huddersfield and South London (Lewisham) where the rector of St Stephens is the Archbishop of Canterbury's visitor to the Windward Island diocese. The USA, particularly New York City, is home to a significant number of Carriacouans. Many Carriacouans do return for holidays or to retire "back home".

Cotton was the leading product to be export during the 18th century.

Carriacou was part of the French colony in 1762. It was part of the British Grenada colony from 1763–1779 and 1783–1974. It was part of French Grenada colony from 1779–1783. It has been a dependency of Grenada since 1974.

Petite Martinique

The first European founder of the island of Petite Martinique was a French Fisherman called Mr. Pierre from Martinique. It is thought that he figured that the isle was shaped roughly like Martinique so he named it *Petit* (little) Martinique.

Recent history

The majority of the inhabitants today are of African descent. There still is a British influence on the island as it was colonised by the British Empire and it is part of Grenada, a Commonwealth state. There is still a French influence which is demonstrated in village names, such as L'Esterre, La Resource, Beausejour, et cetera, and the local patois is still spoken.

The Sacred Heart Church was the first Roman Catholic church on the of Petite Martinique and the first wooden building. It was destroyed by a hurricane in the 1940s and the Church standing today was built in the 1947.

Though Hurricane Ivan in 2004 dealt a devastating blow to the island of Grenada, remarkably, Carriacou and Petite Martinique suffered significantly less damage. However, in 2005, Hurricane Emily hit Carriacou, damaging and forcing evacuation of its only hospital and destroying or damaging hundreds of homes.

Festivals

There are three major cultural festivals held on Carriacou. **Carnival** (see external link below) is held in February or early March. The **Carriacou Regatta**, held on the first weekend in August, is a racing event for locally built boats. In 2005, the Regatta celebrated its 40th anniversary. The **Parang** on the weekend prior to Christmas celebrates the island's traditional Christmas music and culture. Village Maroons all year round and Since the turn of the millennium, a new festival of growing popularity has been started the Carriacou Maroon Festival held during the second quarter of the year.

National Icon

Carriacou

National	Icon
Dish	Coo-coo and Ocra
Plant	Delonix regia
Tree	Flamboyant
Drink	Jack Iron
Telephone company	Cable & Wireless
Bank	Republic Bank
Hospital	Princess Royal Hospital
Real Estate	Carriacou Real Estate

Transport

The people of Carriacou travel mainly by privately run 15 seater buses. Rental cars and taxis are also available and boats are commonplace. There is a small airport Lauriston Airport on the island of Carriacou and a small ferry boat known as the *"Osprey"* that runs between Carriacou, Grenada and Petite Martinique. The short distances between the Grenadines enables travel between them by small boats.

Climate

Dry season is from January to June and the rainy season is from July to December.

Carriacou

	Celsius °C	**Fahrenheit °F**
Land	27-32	80-85
Sea	26-30	78-82

Petite Martinique

	Celsius °C	**Fahrenheit °F**
Land	27-32°C	80-85°F
Sea	26-30°C	78-82°F

In Literature

Carriacou plays a central role in Paule Marshall's novel *"Praisesong for the Widow."* The memory of Carriacou (from which her parents emigrated to New York) figures prominently in Audre Lorde's autobiographical work Zami: A New Spelling of My Name.

Radio

- KYAK106 - Carriacou's Home Grown Radio Station.[3]
- The Harbor Light of the Windwards is a local Christian radio station.[4]

Panorama

External links

- Carriacou Regatta Festival [5]
- CarriacouCam view of Petit Martinique from Belair [6]

See also

- Grenada
- St Vincent and the Grenadines
- Rough Science

Geographical coordinates: 12°29′N 61°28′W

Sauteurs

Sauteurs	
— Town —	
Sauteurs	

Sauteurs	
Location within Grenada	
Coordinates: 12°13′06″N 61°38′21″W	
Country	Grenada
Parish	Saint Patrick
Elevation	285 ft (87 m)
Population (1999)	
- Total	1300
Time zone	UTC-4

Sauteurs (pronounced Sau-tez) is a Fishing Town in the Saint Patrick Parish, Grenada and is the sixth largest in Grenada, with a population of about 1,300. It is located in the far north of that island overlooking Sauteurs Bay. It's the largest town in the north of Grenada and it is the capital of Saint Patrick Parish, Grenada.

History

Here, the last remaining Carib Natives in Grenada jumped off a 40-meter-tall cliff later named Caribs' Leap to their deaths in 1651 rather than face domination by the conquering French. Thus the town was named *Sauteurs*, which is French for "jumpers". The trees and grotto erected in 1664 by Dominican Fathers to make a souls for Caribs and their place are a wooden deck from the century to today. The St Patrick's Catholic church were founded in 1721 but in 1784 the British government handed the church to St Patrick's Anglican church but the church was destroyed by fire and is a police station today. In 1840 the St Patrick Catholic church were construction and today the church is present in Sauteurs.

Images

Saint Mark Parish, Grenada

Saint Mark Parish	
— Parish —	
St Mark Parish Sign	

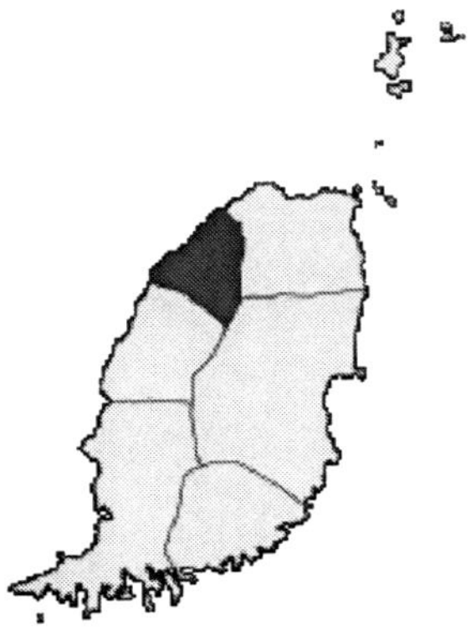

Country	Grenada
Capital City	Victoria
Area	
- Total	9 sq mi (23 km^2)
Population	
- Total	3,994
- Density	409.2/sq mi (158/km^2)

St Mark Parish is a parish on the west coast of Grenada. It is the smallest parish on the island.

Victoria

Along the west coast of the island nation of Grenada lies the small fishing village of Victoria, Grenada. Victoria is the center of activity for the St. Mark's parish, the smallest parish on the island in both area and populace with approximately 4,000 people residing. Local activities include the Saint Mark's fiesta which showcases different produce, foods, culture, music and entertainment throughout the villages of St. Mark. St. Mark's Day is usually a few weeks after Easter in mid April.

Topography

St Mark's has the highest mountain on Grenada, Mount Saint Catherine, and the tallest waterfall, the Tufton Hall Waterfall.

Food Fest

The village of Victoria has created a monthly event called the "Sunset City Food Fest." This activity has been created to improve the living conditions of the people of Victoria and have created a common location where the community can come together to enjoy quality food, time and company. It was set up in 2007 in response to of 250 jobs in he nutmeg industry caused by the effects of hurricane Ivan. Thus far the Food Fest is on the last Saturday of each month, however, it is currently aiming to take place fortnightly.

Vendors offer Grenadian cuisine using local ingredients. Dishes include bakes, figs, breadfruit, Farine, Jacks and other Fish, the Grenada Oil-Down, rotis, calaloo soup, crabs, conches (lambi), Tania Log (a porridge prepared from root crops in a traditional manner), and ice cream.

Constituency

Geographical coordinates: 12°11′N 61°42′W

Attractions

Mount Saint Catherine (Grenada)

Mount Saint Catherine	

Mount Saint Catherine

Elevation	840 m (2756 ft)
Prominence	840 m (2756 ft)
Location	
Coordinates	12°9′00″N 61°40′12″W
Geology	
Type	Stratovolcano
Last eruption	Unknown

Mount Saint Catherine is a stratovolcano and the highest mountain on the Caribbean island of Grenada. It is located in St. Mark's, Victoria. It is the youngest of five volcanoes which comprise the island. The volcano has a horseshoe-shaped crater open to the east, with several lava domes within it. Guides from Victoria are ready and able to take visitors to the top of the mountain or even to the Tufton Hall Waterfall for a look at the largest waterfall on the island.

See also

- List of volcanoes in Grenada

References

- "St. Catherine" [1]. Global Volcanism Program, Smithsonian Institution.

Kick-'em-Jenny

Kick-'em-Jenny

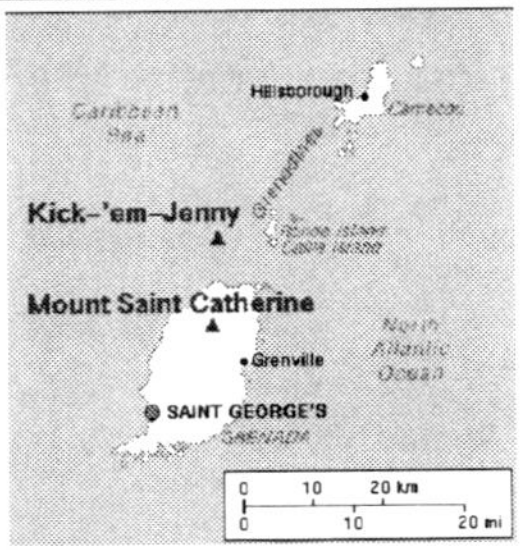

Location map of submarine volcano Kick-'em-Jenny

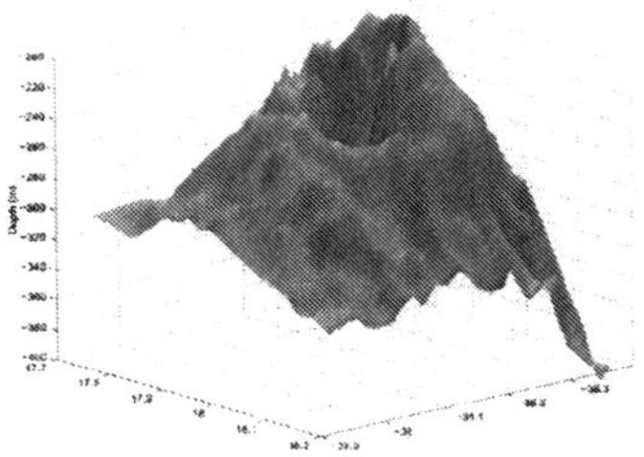

Summit depth	-180 m (−591 ft)
Height	1300 m (4265 ft)
Location	
Location	Caribbean Sea, north of Grenada
Coordinates	12°18′N 61°38′W
Geology	
Type	Submarine volcano (seamount)
Last eruption	2001

Kick-'em-Jenny (also: **Kick'em Jenny** or **Mt. Kick-'Em-Jenny**) is an active submarine volcano or seamount on the Caribbean Sea floor, located 8 km (5 mi) north of the island of Grenada and about 8 km (5 mi) west of Ronde Island in the Grenadines. Kick-'em-Jenny rises 1300 m (4265 ft) above the sea floor on the steep inner western slope of the Lesser Antilles ridge. The North American tectonic plate is subducting the Caribbean tectonic plate to the east of this ridge and under the Lesser Antilles island arc.

Activity

The first record of the volcano was in 1939, although it must have erupted many times before that date. On 23-24 July 1939 an eruption broke the sea surface, sending a cloud of steam and debris 275 m (902 ft) into the air and generating a series of tsunamis around two metres high when they reached the coastlines of northern Grenada and the southern Grenadines. In 2003, the summit reached 180 m (591 ft) below the sea surface and is thought to have remained constant since the 1960s.

The volcano has erupted on at least twelve occasions since 1939 and 2001 (the last being on December 4, 2001), although none of the eruptions have been as large as the 1939 one and most were only detected seismically. The larger eruptions have also been heard underwater or on land close to the volcano as a deep rumbling sound.

A submersible survey in 2003 detected a crater with active fumaroles releasing cold and hot gas bubbles. Samples of fresh olivine basalt were collected. An arc shaped collapse structure appears on the west flank and was the apparent source of a submarine debris avalanche extending 15 km down the ridge slope to the west toward the Grenada Basin.

Etymology

The volcano was unknown before 1939, although "Kick 'em Jenny" appeared on earlier maps as either the name of a small island now called Diamond Rock (or Île Diamante), or the name of the strait between Grenada and Ronde Island (or Île de Ronde). The name itself may be a reference to the waters sometimes being extremely rough.

See also

- List of volcanoes in Grenada

Willis, Grenada

Willis	
— Village —	

Willis
Location within Grenada

Coordinates: 12°05′N 61°43′W	
Country	Grenada
Parish	Saint George
Elevation	1053 ft (321 m)
Population	
- Total	500
Time zone	UTC-4

Willis is a town in Grenada; it is located some miles inland from Saint George's, towards the center of the island. It is the community where the famous Annandale Waterfalls is eloquently situated. With lush evergreen trees, unusually- never before seen exotic plants and an array of spices and fruit trees live here.

Willis has traditionally been a large village with a population of over five thousand (5000) residents. It has been noted from the most recent evaluation census, that is the second largest largest village in Grenada following the village of Marquis, in St. Andrews.

Tufton Hall Waterfall

The **Tufton Hall Waterfall** is located in St. Mark's, Victoria, Grenada. It is the tallest waterfall on Grenada. The only way to visit the waterfall is to hike for approximately 3 hours through technical terrain.

Grenville, Grenada

Grenville	
— Town —	
Nickname(s): La Bay, Rainbow City	

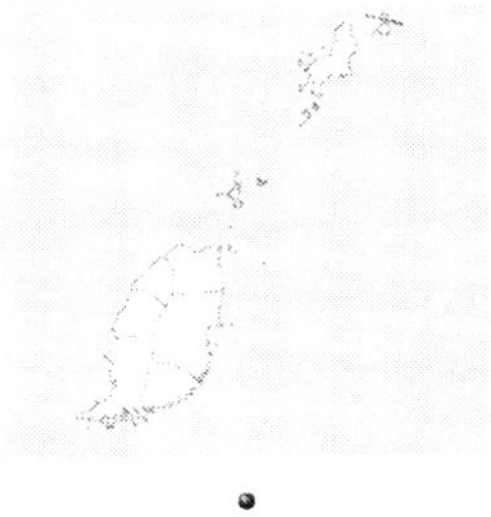

Grenville

Location within Grenada

Coordinates: 12°07′09″N 61°37′35″W	
Country	Grenada
Parish	Saint Andrew
Elevation	0 ft (0 m)
Population	
- Total	2400
Time zone	UTC-4

Grenville is the second largest city in Grenada, after St. George's, and it is the capital of the largest parish, Saint Andrew Parish. Grenville is located on Grenville Bay, about halfway up the east coast of the Caribbean island of Grenada and is heavily involved in the agriculture export industry. Grenville's Anglican Church and school stand at the north end of Victoria Street, the main thoroughfare along the bay.

The city has a population of about 2,400 residents, with many more in the surrounding region. It serves as an economic and transportation hub for that part of the island, having the largest nutmeg-processing plant in Grenada. From the city's marketplace you can find minibuses (the common form of public transportation on the island) to areas all around the island. It is located near Grenada's first airport, Pearls Airport, which became disused when a new airport was built.

Eric Gairy, the first Prime Minister of Grenada, was born near Grenville.

History

Founded and named for George Grenville (British Prime Minister, 1763-65). It was the Parish Capital since 1796. Grenville has had a Court House on Sandel Street since c.1886. In 1981 Grenville Magistrate Court was built.

References

- Grenada - Explorations [1]

Ronde Island

Ronde Island, Grenada is a 2000-acre (8.1 km^2) private island in the Lesser Antilles chain of the Caribbean Sea. The island was listed for sale as of October of 2007 for US$100,000,000, making it currently the most expensive listed island property in the world. Ronde is located approximately 4 miles east of the active submarine volcano Kick-'em-Jenny.

See also

- List of islands in the Caribbean

Saint David Parish, Grenada

St. David Parish	
— Parish —	
Nickname(s): The Virgin Parish	

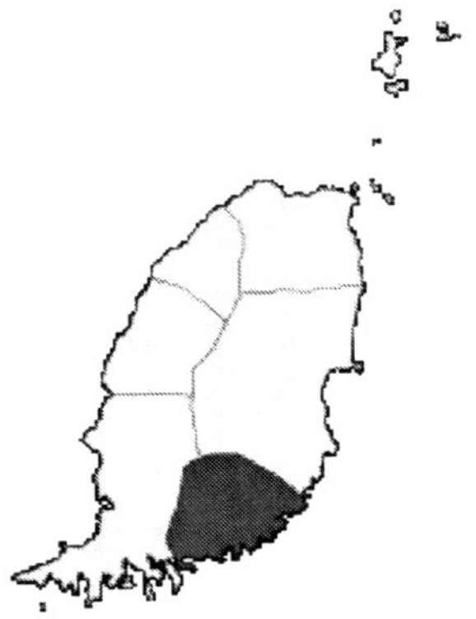

Country	Grenada
Capital City	
Area	
- Total	18 sq mi (47 km^2)
Population	
- Total	11,486
- Density	676/sq mi (261/km^2)

Saint David in the southeastern part of Grenada is the fourth largest parish on the island. It is also the only one without a main town. Because of this fact, it is sometimes referred to as "The Virgin Parish". It is ringed by spectacular bays and inlets that help to provide the nation with a variety of small secluded beaches. With a rocky coastline that slopes up gently towards the central mountainous ridge, its beauty lies in its completely rural state.

History

A town called Megrin was established at St David's Point in 1609 and destroyed during the 1795-1796 by Fedon conflict and the town never built. In the 1721 the catholic parish of Megrin was re open by the French, but it was built down next to the sea. In 1747 Megrin in St David was one of the six churches and parishes in Grenada. In 1795 the Fedon Rebellion became a battle between Fedon and the

English troops stay at the church over night.

External links

Geographical coordinates: 12°03′46″N 61°39′38″W

Gouyave

Gouyave	
— Town —	

Gouyave Welcome Sign

Nickname(s): Action City
The Town That Never Sleeps

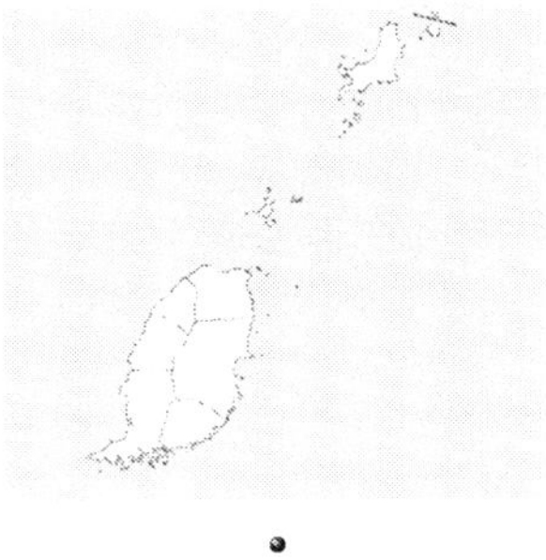

Gouyave

Location within Grenada

Coordinates: 12°09′59″N 61°43′48″W	
Country	Grenada
Parish	Saint John
Government	
- Representative	Michael Church
Elevation	269 ft (82 m)
Population (2008)	
- Total	4378
	city proper
Time zone	UTC-4
Website	Official website [1]

Gouyave is the third-largest fishing town in Grenada (behind the capital, St. George's, with a population of 4,378. It is located on the west coast of the Grenada and is the capital of the Saint John Parish.

Gouyave is known as, "the town that never sleeps" and does a fine job living up to its name. It is also called the "action city", and is known for its social events, festivals, (fish friday), carnival, and dances/party.

Gouyave was just a subsistence economy of poor fishermen and rural nutmeg/cocoa farmers, but has blossomed into a cosmopolitan town with fine houses, glittering bars, clubs, attractive nightlife, appealing festivals, and a reputation for its entertainment.

History

Originally called Charlotte Town after Queen Charlotte of Britain, it was renamed Gouyave by the French because of its large amounts of guava trees. The town was the site of a large battle, on Tuesday March 1795, between Captain Guerdon and Fedon and there were 30 people in this battle. On the 3rd of December 1882, the largest wooden Jetty ever built in Grenada, it was opened and took place in this town. In August 1888 the saving bank was opened in Gouyave. In July 1890, Gouyave water work was opened. On the 15th of November 1896, the river in Gouyave was seriously damage by flood. On the 6th of August 1899, the Gouyave Anglican church was struck by lighting.

Culture

One of the town's annual celebrations is Fisherman's Birthday, also known as "29th June". On the day of June 29, fishermen come from all over Grenada for competitive boat racing, entertainment, fish foods, and many other activities. Also, every Friday the town celebrates "Fish Friday", a warm atmosphere of locals and tourists socializing and eating all sorts of fish dishes and meals.

Fish Friday is a weekly festival that offers a wide range of food (fish) and entertainment. Fish Friday was founded to promote community development in Gouyave and in the overall Parish of St. John's by promoting Gouyave as a "Fish Village".

Neighbourhoods and Districts/Suburbs

- Upper Depradine street

    a) Lance
    b) Hills View
    c) Victoria Road(Crapo Street)
    d) Edward Street
    e) Langton Road

f) Boyke's Lane
g) New Street
h) Chapel lane
i) River Lane
j) Ottley's lane

- Central Depradine street

a) St. Dominic's Street
b) St. Francis Street
c) School Lane
d) Cornet Walk

- Lower Depradine street

a) St. Peter's Street
b) Ferguson's Lane
c) St. Benoit Street

- Harlem
- Loretto
- Florida
- Gouyave-estate

a) Central
b) Market Square
c) Mongo Road
d) Middle River

- Doctor Belle
- Dougladston
- Clozier
- Maran

External links

- http://www.gogouyave.com

Victoria, Grenada

Victoria	
— Town —	

Victoria

Location within Grenada

Coordinates: 12°11′N 61°42′W	
Country	Grenada
Parish	Saint Mark
Elevation	509 ft (155 m)
Time zone	UTC-4

Victoria is a town in Saint Mark Parish, Grenada. It is located on the island's northwest coast between Gouyave and Nonpareil.[*citation needed*]

Geography

Along the west coast of the island nation of Grenada lies the small fishing village of Victoria. Victoria is the center of activity for the St Mark's parish, the smallest parish on the island in both area and populace with approximately 4,000 people residing. The people of Victoria are warm, kind and very friendly.[*citation needed*] When one lives in Victoria, or St Mark's, they are dubbed to be living in the country. And when you visit, you will most definitely get that feel as you see farmers collecting their produce and the small mom and pop stores surrounding the village.[*citation needed*]

The community enjoys playing and watching football and cricket, "liming" on the streets and bars, and cooking the national dish, Oil Down. Victoria has many night clubs and bars to which anyone can go to enjoy some Clarks Courts or Carib and some great company.[*citation needed*] Every year, Victoria hosts a festival which is called the ST. MARK'S DAY FIESTA which showcases different produce, foods, cultures, music and entertainment throughout the villages of St. Mark. St. Mark's Day is usually a few weeks after Easter in mid April and provides hours of entertainment and excitement.

The village of Victoria has also created a monthly event called the "Sunset City Food Fest." This activity has been created to improve the living conditions of the people of Victoria and have created a common location where the community can come together to enjoy quality food, time and company. Thus far the Food Fest is on the last Saturday of each month, however, is looking to increase its occurrences fortnightly.[*citation needed*]

The village of Victoria is placed in an ideal location to which it receives cool trade winds and is privileged enough to have the highest mountain and waterfall within its parish boundaries. Although St. Mark's may be the smallest parish, it makes up with having the highest mountain (Mount Saint Catherine) and tallest, most beautifully secluded waterfall on the island called "The Tufton Hall Waterfall.[*citation needed*]

In Victoria, one can be entertained in whatever way one is inclined, playing football, cricket, basketball, bathing in the sea, taking a swim in the river, checking out the sulfur springs, hiking Mt. St. Catherine, visiting the Tufton Hall Waterfall, enjoying the atmosphere of the Sunset City Food Fest, and even attending St. Mark's Day for an entire day of enjoyment!

Bianca C

Career	
Name:	*Marechal Petain* (1944-1946) *La Marseillaise* (1946-1957) *Arosa Sky* (1957-1959) *Bianca C* (1959-1961)
Builder:	Construction Navales La Ciotat
Launched:	June 1944
Completed:	July 1949
Fate:	Sunk, 24 October 1961
General characteristics	
Type:	Passenger ship
Tonnage:	gross tonnage (GT) of 18427 tons
Length:	600 ft (180 m)
Capacity:	400 passengers
Crew:	300

The ***Bianca C*** was a passenger ship that sank on two occasions, the first time in France before being completed, and the second time after an explosion and fire off the island of Grenada.

History

Built during World War II at Construction Navales La Ciotat, a shipyard on the southern coast of France, the ship was first launched in June 1944 under the name *Marechal Petain*. Construction had not yet been completed, so the ship was towed to Port de Bouc, near Marseille, where she was torpedoed by the Germans in August. When the hull was raised, it was renamed *La Marseillaise* and towed to Toulon before being returned to La Ciotat to be refitted as a cruise ship. When the remodeling was completed in July 1949, she sailed to Yokohama. In 1957, the ship was given the name *Arosa Sky* after being sold to Panama's Arosa Line. She was refitted again and became the company's flagship, but within two years Arosa Line was forced to sell the ship to Costa Line, an Italian company also known as Linea C. After that 1959 sale, the boat was renamed the *Bianca C* (the second Costa C ship so named) for one of the owner's daughters, and was refurbished once again. The *Bianca C*'s main route ran from Italy to Venezuela, including stops in the Caribbean.

Sinking

On Sunday October 22, 1961, the *Bianca C* was ten days out of Naples and docked off Grenada when an explosion occurred in the engine room in the early hours of the morning. One crewman died immediately, and eight others were injured. As fires broke out, approximately 700 passengers and crew scrambled to abandon the ship while Grenadian fishermen and boat owners, awakened by the noise of the explosion, near the harbor of St. George's rushed to help. Survivors were taken to the capital, where makeshift hospitals were hastily established to provide shelter and food. Because Grenada did not have the equipment to quench such a large fire, a call for help was sent and was received by the British frigate HMS *Londonderry* at Puerto Rico. It took two days for the *Londonderry* to arrive, and by that time the *Bianca C* had begun to sink. The burning ship was in the main anchorage and would block the harbor if it sank there, so a *Londonderry* boarding party boarded the flaming boat to attach a towline. The anchor lines of the *Bianca C* were burned, and today the anchors are still at the mouth of the St. George's harbor. Meanwhile, the *Londonderry* moved to tow the *Bianca C*, but the latter ship was listing to port. Thousands of Grenadians watched from the mountains as the tow progressed for six hours, but the *Bianca C.* had only moved three miles (5 km) when a squall started and the towline broke. The *Bianca C* sank quickly into 165 feet (50 m) of water, about a mile from the popular tourist beach at Grand Anse.

Wreck

In the 1970s, a Trinidadian firm salvaged the *Bianca C*'s propellers and sold them for scrap. As the top of the ship is in only about 100 feet (30 m) of water, scuba divers can reach it and in the late 1980s and early 1990s some removed parts of the boat for souvenirs. In late 1992, the rear third of the ship was torn off and the ship began to deteriorate quickly, though at 600 feet (180 m) in length it is still the region's largest shipwreck. A bronze statue of Christ of the Abyss was given by the Costa Line to Grenada in appreciation of the country's hospitality, and the statue stands in the Carenage surrounding the harbor at St. George's.

The Times named the *Bianca C* as one of the top ten wreck diving sites in the world.

See also

- List of ship launches in 1944
- List of shipwrecks in 1944
- List of shipwrecks in 1961

References

- Caribbean Diving Grenada - the Bianca C [1]
- Dive Grenada [2]
- Costa Line - Linea "C" Page 1A - The Early Liners 1948-65 [3] - Retrieved June 30, 2007

External links

- Bianca C. postcards [3]
- Sculpture Christ of the Deep [4]

Queen's Park, Grenada

Ground information	
Location	Grenada
Establishment	2007
Capacity	20,000
Owner	West Indies Cricket Board

As of March 19 2009
Source: Cricinfo [1]

Cricket National Stadium, previously known as, Queen's Park, is the name of a cricket stadium complex in River Road, Grenada in the Caribbean and was a location for the 2007 Cricket World Cup.

After being rebuilt in 2000, the new complex was badly damaged in October 2004 from a direct hit by Hurricane Ivan. The pitch is noted for being elongated towards the Pavilion end, giving a more baseball type look to the ground. The stadium was funded by the People's Republic of China.

See also

- Cricket
- 2007 cricket World Cup
- List of Test cricket grounds

After the success of its use in the world cup, the stadium has been used recently for youth games in the country including matches against touring sides from England

External links

- *Hurricane Destroys Grenada Stadium* [2] News article at caribbeancricket.com

Geographical coordinates: 12°3′32.6″N 61°45′7.6″W

Transportation

Maurice Bishop International Airport

Maurice Bishop International Airport

IATA: GND – ICAO: TGPY

Maurice Bishop International Airport
Location of airport in Grenada

Summary	
Airport type	Public
Operator	Grenada Airports Authority
Location	St. George's, Grenada
Hub for	{{{hub}}}
Elevation AMSL	41 ft / 12 m
Coordinates	12°00′15″N 061°47′10″W
Website	www.mbiagrenada.com [1]

Runways

Direction	**Length**		**Surface**
	ft	**m**	
10/28	9,003	2,744	Asphalt

Source: DAFIF

Maurice Bishop International Airport (IATA: **GND**, ICAO: **TGPY**), formerly known as **Point Salines International Airport**, is located in the parish of St. George's. The town of St. George's is about 5 miles (8.0 km) north of the airport and is the capital of the island nation of Grenada. The airport is located on Point Salines, the most southwestern point of the island.

History

The unfinished airport was chosen as the jump off point for the invasion of the Island by the United States to restore order there after hard-line pro-Communist elements within Grenada's government and military seized power in October 1983. More than 500 Rangers from 1st and 2nd Battalions of the United States Army 75th Ranger Regiment conducted a risky daylight low altitude parachute assault onto the airport. Despite resistance from Grenadian armed forces (PRA - People's Revolutionary Army) and Cuban forces (NOT Cuban regular military forces - but armed construction workers.), the Rangers secured all of their objectives on the airfield quickly. The seizure of the airfield allowed United States Air Force C-141 transport planes to land and unload paratroopers from the 82nd Airborne Division.

The building of the airport — designed to replace the obsolete Pearls Airport on the north side of the island — was cited by U.S. President Ronald Reagan as evidence that the Grenadian government intended to allow it to be used as a way point for Soviet military aircraft en route to Cuba. He buttressed this claim with the evidence that it was being built, in part, by Cuban workers. The contention that the airport had any military function was vehemently denied by Grenada's Prime Minister Maurice Bishop. Bishop and his government contended that the Point Salines airport was intended to make the island more accessible to European and North American tourists. The long range jets that carried such tourists could not land on the short and geographically difficult runway at the existing airport, Pearls. As a result, tourists bound for Grenada had to put up with the delays, expenses and perceived risks of changing to smaller planes flown by regional carriers. The Grenadian government said they hoped their tourist trade would dramatically increase if direct flights from Europe and North America were possible. The airport itself was designed by a Canadian firm and the construction contracts were awarded to mostly European contractors.

The event that precipitated the U.S.-led invasion of Grenada was not the construction of the airport, but, rather, a violent coup in which Prime Minister Bishop was killed. The American justification for the invasion was the perceived threat to American medical students at St. George's University, whose campus is a short distance from the Maurice Bishop International Airport.

Facilities

The airport resides at an elevation of 41 feet (12 m) above mean sea level. It has one runway designated 10/28 with an asphalt surface measuring 9003 by 148 feet (2744 × 45 m).

Airlines and destinations

The following airlines serve Grenada:

Airlines	Destinations
Air Canada	**Seasonal** : Toronto-Pearson
Air Transat	**Seasonal** : Toronto-Pearson
American Airlines	Miami
American Eagle	San Juan
British Airways	Barbados, London-Gatwick
Caribbean Airlines operated by Air Jamaica	New York-JFK
Condor	Frankfurt **Seasonal** : Porlamar
Delta Air Lines	New York-JFK
LIAT	Barbados, Canouan, Port of Spain, St Vincent, Tobago
Monarch Airlines	London-Gatwick
Sunwing Airlines	**Seasonal** : Toronto-Pearson
SVG Air	Canouan, Carriacou, Union Island
Virgin Atlantic Airways	London-Gatwick

Cargo carriers

- Amerijet (Trinidad, Miami, Santiago (DR), Santo Domingo)
- DHL (St.Vincent, Trinidad)
- FedEx (St.Vincent, Aguadilla)
- LIAT Quikpak (St.Vincent, Barbados, Tobago, Trinidad, Canouan)

External links

- Maurice Bishop International Airport [1], official site
- Current weather for TGPY [2] at NOAA/NWS
- Accident history for GND [3] at Aviation Safety Network

Pearls Airport

Pearls Airport	
IATA: *none* – ICAO: TGPG/MKPE	

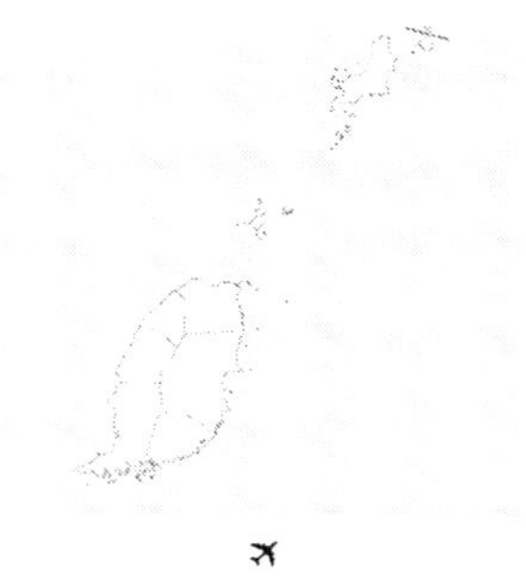

Pearls Airport

Location of airport in Grenada

Summary	
Airport type	Public
Operator	Grenada Airports Authority
Location	Grenville, Grenada
Hub for	{{{hub}}}
Coordinates	12°08′38″N 061°37′01″W

Pearls Airport (ICAO: **TGPG**) was Grenada's first airport. It is currently under the management of the Grenada Airports Authority. The airport is not in daily operation. In 1984 it was replaced as Grenada's main airport by the Point Salines International Airport. It is now a construction site and go-kart track. There is a derelict Cuba airliner still in position by the runway.

External links

- Aerial photo of Pearl's Airport [1] from SVG Air website

Lauriston Airport

Lauriston Airport			
IATA: CRU – ICAO: TGPZ			

Location of airport in Grenada

Summary	
Airport type	Public
Operator	Grenada Airports Authority
Location	Hillsborough, Carriacou, Grenada
Hub for	{{{hub}}}
Elevation AMSL	5 ft / 2 m
Coordinates	12°28′37″N 061°28′20″W

Runways			
Direction	**Length**		**Surface**
	m	**ft**	
09/27	800	2,625	Asphalt

Source: Great Circle Mapper

Lauriston Airport (IATA: **CRU**, ICAO: **TGPZ**) is an airport located west of Hillsborough, the main town on the island of Carriacou in Grenada. It is also known as **Carriacou Island Airport**.

Facilities

The airport resides at an elevation of 5 feet (2 m) above mean sea level. It has one runway which measures 800 by 18 metres (2625 × 59 ft).

Airlines and destinations

The following airlines serve Lauriston Airport:

Airlines	Destinations
SVG Air	Grenada

Article Sources and Contributors

Grenada *Source*: http://en.wikipedia.org/?oldid=390215371 *Contributors*: Tbhotch

History of Grenada *Source*: http://en.wikipedia.org/?oldid=374238529 *Contributors*: Cdogsimmons

Invasion of Grenada *Source*: http://en.wikipedia.org/?oldid=388213669 *Contributors*: Lionelag

Geography of Grenada *Source*: http://en.wikipedia.org/?oldid=369244202 *Contributors*: Plastikspork

Politics of Grenada *Source*: http://en.wikipedia.org/?oldid=362703560 *Contributors*: 1 anonymous edits

Commonwealth realm *Source*: http://en.wikipedia.org/?oldid=390589973 *Contributors*: 1 anonymous edits

Economy of Grenada *Source*: http://en.wikipedia.org/?oldid=380051603 *Contributors*: Akerans

Culture of Grenada *Source*: http://en.wikipedia.org/?oldid=371568109 *Contributors*:

Music of Grenada *Source*: http://en.wikipedia.org/?oldid=379611657 *Contributors*: Beetstra

List of birds of Grenada *Source*: http://en.wikipedia.org/?oldid=384168886 *Contributors*:

St. George's, Grenada *Source*: http://en.wikipedia.org/?oldid=386897655 *Contributors*: Metallurgist

Saint George Parish, Grenada *Source*: http://en.wikipedia.org/?oldid=359305727 *Contributors*: Kylekieran

Parishes of Grenada *Source*: http://en.wikipedia.org/?oldid=385524016 *Contributors*: Caribbean historian

Saint Andrew Parish, Grenada *Source*: http://en.wikipedia.org/?oldid=355823534 *Contributors*:

Saint John Parish, Grenada *Source*: http://en.wikipedia.org/?oldid=387704055 *Contributors*:

Saint Patrick Parish, Grenada *Source*: http://en.wikipedia.org/?oldid=383088077 *Contributors*: Kylekieran

Amber Belair *Source*: http://en.wikipedia.org/?oldid=366583648 *Contributors*:

Bacolet, Grenada *Source*: http://en.wikipedia.org/?oldid=366583660 *Contributors*:

Barique *Source*: http://en.wikipedia.org/?oldid=366583667 *Contributors*:

Becke Moui *Source*: http://en.wikipedia.org/?oldid=366583672 *Contributors*:

Belmont, Grenada *Source*: http://en.wikipedia.org/?oldid=366583678 *Contributors*:

Bogles *Source*: http://en.wikipedia.org/?oldid=367139591 *Contributors*:

Bois de Gannes *Source*: http://en.wikipedia.org/?oldid=366583696 *Contributors*:

Deblando *Source*: http://en.wikipedia.org/?oldid=366583761 *Contributors*:

Diego Piece *Source*: http://en.wikipedia.org/?oldid=366583772 *Contributors*:

Elie Hall *Source*: http://en.wikipedia.org/?oldid=366583781 *Contributors*:

Grand Roy *Source*: http://en.wikipedia.org/?oldid=366583799 *Contributors*:

Ka-fe Beau *Source*: http://en.wikipedia.org/?oldid=366583835 *Contributors*:

L'Anse Aux Epines *Source*: http://en.wikipedia.org/?oldid=366583844 *Contributors*:

Mamma Cannes *Source*: http://en.wikipedia.org/?oldid=366583848 *Contributors*:

Marquis, Grenada *Source*: http://en.wikipedia.org/?oldid=366583854 *Contributors*:

Maulti *Source*: http://en.wikipedia.org/?oldid=366583861 *Contributors*:

Morne Docteur *Source*: http://en.wikipedia.org/?oldid=366583872 *Contributors*:

Morne Fendue *Source*: http://en.wikipedia.org/?oldid=366583880 *Contributors*:

Morne Jaloux Ridge *Source*: http://en.wikipedia.org/?oldid=366583896 *Contributors*:

Morne Jaloux *Source*: http://en.wikipedia.org/?oldid=366583892 *Contributors*:

Morne Longue *Source*: http://en.wikipedia.org/?oldid=366583908 *Contributors*:

Morne Rouge *Source*: http://en.wikipedia.org/?oldid=366583916 *Contributors*:

Morne Tranquille *Source*: http://en.wikipedia.org/?oldid=366583918 *Contributors*:

Mount Craven *Source*: http://en.wikipedia.org/?oldid=366583930 *Contributors*:

Paradise, Grenada *Source*: http://en.wikipedia.org/?oldid=366583942 *Contributors*:

St. David's, Grenada *Source*: http://en.wikipedia.org/?oldid=366583969 *Contributors*:

Tivoli, Grenada *Source*: http://en.wikipedia.org/?oldid=382558108 *Contributors*:

Union Village, Grenada *Source*: http://en.wikipedia.org/?oldid=366583987 *Contributors*:

Union, Grenada *Source*: http://en.wikipedia.org/?oldid=366583993 *Contributors*:

Upper La Tante *Source*: http://en.wikipedia.org/?oldid=366584053 *Contributors*:

Upper Capitol *Source*: http://en.wikipedia.org/?oldid=366584005 *Contributors*:

Upper Conference *Source*: http://en.wikipedia.org/?oldid=366584046 *Contributors*:

Upper La Taste *Source*: http://en.wikipedia.org/?oldid=366584062 *Contributors*:

Upper Pearls *Source*: http://en.wikipedia.org/?oldid=366584067 *Contributors*:

Hillsborough, Carriacou *Source*: http://en.wikipedia.org/?oldid=367139593 *Contributors*:

Carriacou and Petite Martinique *Source*: http://en.wikipedia.org/?oldid=386034773 *Contributors*: Hmains

Sauteurs *Source*: http://en.wikipedia.org/?oldid=370329932 *Contributors*: Grutness

Saint Mark Parish, Grenada *Source*: http://en.wikipedia.org/?oldid=365814712 *Contributors*: Itsmejudith

Mount Saint Catherine (Grenada) *Source*: http://en.wikipedia.org/?oldid=355883817 *Contributors*: Droll

Kick-'em-Jenny *Source*: http://en.wikipedia.org/?oldid=389386120 *Contributors*: Krenakarore

Willis, Grenada *Source*: http://en.wikipedia.org/?oldid=366584083 *Contributors*:

Tufton Hall Waterfall *Source*: http://en.wikipedia.org/?oldid=377195262 *Contributors*:

Grenville, Grenada *Source*: http://en.wikipedia.org/?oldid=384600808 *Contributors*:

Ronde Island *Source*: http://en.wikipedia.org/?oldid=379486360 *Contributors*: Belgian man

Saint David Parish, Grenada *Source*: http://en.wikipedia.org/?oldid=375470179 *Contributors*:

Gouyave *Source*: http://en.wikipedia.org/?oldid=383293093 *Contributors*: 1 anonymous edits

Victoria, Grenada *Source*: http://en.wikipedia.org/?oldid=366584078 *Contributors*:

Bianca C *Source*: http://en.wikipedia.org/?oldid=373144588 *Contributors*: Dawkeye

Queen's Park, Grenada *Source*: http://en.wikipedia.org/?oldid=340321929 *Contributors*: Karyasuman

Maurice Bishop International Airport *Source*: http://en.wikipedia.org/?oldid=389748451 *Contributors*: 1 anonymous edits

Pearls Airport *Source*: http://en.wikipedia.org/?oldid=349695080 *Contributors*: Kylekieran

Lauriston Airport *Source*: http://en.wikipedia.org/?oldid=365258334 *Contributors*: Belgian man

Image Sources, Licenses and Contributors

File:Flag of Grenada.svg *Source*: http://bibliocm.bibliolabs.com/mwAnon/index.php?title=File:Flag_of_Grenada.svg *License*: Public Domain *Contributors*: User:SKopp

File:LocationGrenada.png *Source*: http://bibliocm.bibliolabs.com/mwAnon/index.php?title=File:LocationGrenada.png *License*: Public Domain *Contributors*: User:Vardion

File:Speaker Icon.svg *Source*: http://bibliocm.bibliolabs.com/mwAnon/index.php?title=File:Speaker_Icon.svg *License*: Public Domain *Contributors*: Blast, G.Hagedorn, Mobius, 2 anonymous edits

File:StGeorgesGrenada2000.jpg *Source*: http://bibliocm.bibliolabs.com/mwAnon/index.php?title=File:StGeorgesGrenada2000.jpg *License*: GNU Free Documentation License *Contributors*: Foroa, Infrogmation, Scanlan, Yrithinnd

File:Eastern Caribbean Defense Force.jpg *Source*: http://bibliocm.bibliolabs.com/mwAnon/index.php?title=File:Eastern_Caribbean_Defense_Force.jpg *License*: Public Domain *Contributors*: TSGT M. J. Creen

File:Grenada-map.png *Source*: http://bibliocm.bibliolabs.com/mwAnon/index.php?title=File:Grenada-map.png *License*: Public Domain *Contributors*: CIA

File:Carriacou Scene.jpg *Source*: http://bibliocm.bibliolabs.com/mwAnon/index.php?title=File:Carriacou_Scene.jpg *License*: unknown *Contributors*: Original uploader was Atiemann at en.wikipedia

File:Grenada parishes named.png *Source*: http://bibliocm.bibliolabs.com/mwAnon/index.php?title=File:Grenada_parishes_named.png *License*: Attribution *Contributors*: User:Golbez

File:Grenada ivan.jpg *Source*: http://bibliocm.bibliolabs.com/mwAnon/index.php?title=File:Grenada_ivan.jpg *License*: unknown *Contributors*: USAID

File:SchoolOnBeach Grenada1965.jpg *Source*: http://bibliocm.bibliolabs.com/mwAnon/index.php?title=File:SchoolOnBeach_Grenada1965.jpg *License*: Creative Commons Attribution-Sharealike 2.5 *Contributors*: User:Infrogmation

File:GrenadaCarnival1965FeatheredHeaddresses.jpg *Source*: http://bibliocm.bibliolabs.com/mwAnon/index.php?title=File:GrenadaCarnival1965FeatheredHeaddresses.jpg *License*: Creative Commons Attribution-Sharealike 2.5 *Contributors*: Infrogmation

File:CH-53D HMM-261 Grenada Okt1983.jpeg *Source*: http://bibliocm.bibliolabs.com/mwAnon/index.php?title=File:CH-53D_HMM-261_Grenada_Okt1983.jpeg *License*: Public Domain *Contributors*: photographer: TSgt. M. J. Creen, USMC

File:Flag of the United States.svg *Source*: http://bibliocm.bibliolabs.com/mwAnon/index.php?title=File:Flag_of_the_United_States.svg *License*: Public Domain *Contributors*: User:Dbenbenn, User:Indolences, User:Jacobolus, User:Technion, User:Zscout370

File:Flag of Antigua and Barbuda.svg *Source*: http://bibliocm.bibliolabs.com/mwAnon/index.php?title=File:Flag of Antigua and Barbuda.svg *License*: Public Domain *Contributors*: User:Dbenbenn

File:Flag of Barbados.svg *Source*: http://bibliocm.bibliolabs.com/mwAnon/index.php?title=File:Flag_of_Barbados.svg *License*: Public Domain *Contributors*: User:Denelson83

File:Flag of Dominica 1981.svg *Source*: http://bibliocm.bibliolabs.com/mwAnon/index.php?title=File:Flag_of_Dominica_1981.svg *License*: Public Domain *Contributors*: User:Himasaram

File:Flag of Jamaica.svg *Source*: http://bibliocm.bibliolabs.com/mwAnon/index.php?title=File:Flag_of_Jamaica.svg *License*: Public Domain *Contributors*: User:Madden

File:Flag of Saint Lucia (1979-2002).svg *Source*: http://bibliocm.bibliolabs.com/mwAnon/index.php?title=File:Flag_of_Saint_Lucia_(1979-2002).svg *License*: Public Domain *Contributors*: Permjak, Raymond, Zscout370

File:Flag of Saint Vincent and the Grenadines (1979).png *Source*: http://bibliocm.bibliolabs.com/mwAnon/index.php?title=File:Flag_of_Saint_Vincent_and_the_Grenadines_(1979).png *License*: Public Domain *Contributors*: Original uploader was Orange Tuesday at en.wikipedia (Original text : Orange Tuesday (talk))

File:Flag of Cuba.svg *Source*: http://bibliocm.bibliolabs.com/mwAnon/index.php?title=File:Flag_of_Cuba.svg *License*: Public Domain *Contributors*: see below

File:M102 howitzers during Operation Urgent Fury.jpg *Source*: http://bibliocm.bibliolabs.com/mwAnon/index.php?title=File:M102_howitzers_during_Operation_Urgent_Fury.jpg *License*: Public Domain *Contributors*: TSGT M. J. CREEN

File:Urgent fury civilians waiting.jpg *Source*: http://bibliocm.bibliolabs.com/mwAnon/index.php?title=File:Urgent fury civilians waiting.jpg *License*: Public Domain *Contributors*: TSGT M. J. CREEN

File:BTR-60PB Urgent Fury.jpg *Source*: http://bibliocm.bibliolabs.com/mwAnon/index.php?title=File:BTR-60PB_Urgent_Fury.jpg *License*: Public Domain *Contributors*: Not listed

File:AH-1S firing cannon Grenada 1983.JPEG *Source*: http://bibliocm.bibliolabs.com/mwAnon/index.php?title=File:AH-1S_firing_cannon_Grenada_1983.JPEG *License*: Public Domain *Contributors*: MSgt. David Goldie

File:Explosion2 during Grenada invasion 1983.JPEG *Source*: http://bibliocm.bibliolabs.com/mwAnon/index.php?title=File:Explosion2_during_Grenada_invasion_1983.JPEG *License*: Public Domain *Contributors*: Spec. Long

File:Grenada Invasion.jpg *Source*: http://bibliocm.bibliolabs.com/mwAnon/index.php?title=File:Grenada_Invasion.jpg *License*: Public Domain *Contributors*: United States Military Academy

File:A-7E over Port Salines airfield Grenada 1983.jpg *Source*: http://bibliocm.bibliolabs.com/mwAnon/index.php?title=File:A-7E over Port Salines airfield Grenada 1983.jpg *License*: Public Domain *Contributors*: USN

File:Grenada barracks before and after attack 1983.jpg *Source*: http://bibliocm.bibliolabs.com/mwAnon/index.php?title=File:Grenada_barracks_before_and_after_attack_1983.jpg *License*: Public Domain *Contributors*: USN

File:USPlanGrenadaUrgentFury.jpg *Source*: http://bibliocm.bibliolabs.com/mwAnon/index.php?title=File:USPlanGrenadaUrgentFury.jpg *License*: Public Domain *Contributors*: John M. Shalikashvili, Joint Chiefs of Staff uploaded by Wikifreund

Image:Gj-map.gif *Source*: http://bibliocm.bibliolabs.com/mwAnon/index.php?title=File:Gj-map.gif *License*: Public Domain *Contributors*: Arb, Kintetsubuffalo, PoM, Ras67, Telim tor

File:LocationRonde.PNG *Source*: http://bibliocm.bibliolabs.com/mwAnon/index.php?title=File:LocationRonde.PNG *License*: Public Domain *Contributors*: User:Rémih

Image:Grenada.png *Source*: http://bibliocm.bibliolabs.com/mwAnon/index.php?title=File:Grenada.png *License*: Public Domain *Contributors*: Bollar, Smiley, Telim tor, Verdy p, 1 anonymous edits

Image:PD-icon.svg *Source*: http://bibliocm.bibliolabs.com/mwAnon/index.php?title=File:PD-icon.svg *License*: Public Domain *Contributors*: User:Duesentrieb, User:Rfl

File:Commonwealth realms map.svg *Source*: http://bibliocm.bibliolabs.com/mwAnon/index.php?title=File:Commonwealth_realms_map.svg *License*: Public Domain *Contributors*: User:Applysense

File:Flag of Australia.svg *Source*: http://bibliocm.bibliolabs.com/mwAnon/index.php?title=File:Flag_of_Australia.svg *License*: Public Domain *Contributors*: Ian Fieggen

Image:Royal Standard of Australia.svg *Source*: http://bibliocm.bibliolabs.com/mwAnon/index.php?title=File:Royal_Standard_of_Australia.svg *License*: GNU Free Documentation License *Contributors*: user:Editor at Large

File:Flag of the Bahamas.svg *Source*: http://bibliocm.bibliolabs.com/mwAnon/index.php?title=File:Flag_of_the_Bahamas.svg *License*: Public Domain *Contributors*: Bahamas government

Image:Royal Standard of Barbados.svg *Source*: http://bibliocm.bibliolabs.com/mwAnon/index.php?title=File:Royal_Standard_of_Barbados.svg *License*: GNU Free Documentation License *Contributors*: User:Barryob

File:Flag of Belize.svg *Source*: http://bibliocm.bibliolabs.com/mwAnon/index.php?title=File:Flag_of_Belize.svg *License*: Public Domain *Contributors*: Caleb Moore

File:Flag of Canada.svg *Source*: http://bibliocm.bibliolabs.com/mwAnon/index.php?title=File:Flag_of_Canada.svg *License*: Public Domain *Contributors*: User:E Pluribus Anthony, User:Mzajac

Image:Royal Standard of Canada.svg *Source*: http://bibliocm.bibliolabs.com/mwAnon/index.php?title=File:Royal_Standard_of_Canada.svg *License*: Public Domain *Contributors*: User:....

Image:Royal Standard of Jamaica.svg *Source*: http://bibliocm.bibliolabs.com/mwAnon/index.php?title=File:Royal_Standard_of_Jamaica.svg *License*: GNU Free Documentation License *Contributors*: User:Barryob

File:Flag of New Zealand.svg *Source*: http://bibliocm.bibliolabs.com/mwAnon/index.php?title=File:Flag_of_New_Zealand.svg *License*: Public Domain *Contributors*: Adambro, Arria Belli, Avenue, Bawolff, Bjankuloski06en, ButterStick, Denelson83, Donk, Duduziq, EugeneZelenko, Fred J, Fry1989, Hugh Jass, Ibagli, Jusjih, Klemen Kocjancic, Mamndassan, Mattes, Nightstallion, O, Peeperman, Poromiami, Reisio, Rfc1394, Shizhao, Tabasco, Transparent Blue, Väsk, Xufanc, Zscout370, 35 anonymous edits

Image:Royal Standard of New Zealand.svg *Source*: http://bibliocm.bibliolabs.com/mwAnon/index.php?title=File:Royal_Standard_of_New_Zealand.svg *License*: GNU Free Documentation License *Contributors*: User:Denelson83

File:Flag of Papua New Guinea.svg *Source*: http://bibliocm.bibliolabs.com/mwAnon/index.php?title=File:Flag_of_Papua_New_Guinea.svg *License*: Public Domain *Contributors*: User:Nightstallion

File:Flag of Saint Kitts and Nevis.svg *Source*: http://bibliocm.bibliolabs.com/mwAnon/index.php?title=File:Flag_of_Saint_Kitts_and_Nevis.svg *License*: Public Domain *Contributors*: User:Pumbaa80

File:Flag of Saint Lucia.svg *Source*: http://bibliocm.bibliolabs.com/mwAnon/index.php?title=File:Flag_of_Saint_Lucia.svg *License*: Public Domain *Contributors*: User:SKopp

File:Flag of Saint Vincent and the Grenadines.svg *Source*: http://bibliocm.bibliolabs.com/mwAnon/index.php?title=File:Flag_of_Saint_Vincent_and_the_Grenadines.svg *License*: Public Domain *Contributors*: User:SKopp

File:Flag of the Solomon Islands.svg *Source*: http://bibliocm.bibliolabs.com/mwAnon/index.php?title=File:Flag_of_the_Solomon_Islands.svg *License*: Public Domain *Contributors*: User:SKopp

File:Flag of Tuvalu.svg *Source*: http://bibliocm.bibliolabs.com/mwAnon/index.php?title=File:Flag_of_Tuvalu.svg *License*: Public Domain *Contributors*: Avala, CommonsDelinker, Davepape, Denelson83, DiamondVertex, Fry1989, Greentubing, Homo lupus, Jed, Klemen Kocjancic, Kookaburra, Mattes, Neq00, Nightstallion, Vzb83, 8 anonymous edits

File:Flag of the United Kingdom.svg *Source*: http://bibliocm.bibliolabs.com/mwAnon/index.php?title=File:Flag_of_the_United_Kingdom.svg *License*: Public Domain *Contributors*: User:Zscout370

Image:Royal Standard of the United Kingdom.svg *Source*: http://bibliocm.bibliolabs.com/mwAnon/index.php?title=File:Royal_Standard_of_the_United_Kingdom.svg *License*: GNU Free Documentation License *Contributors*: User:Barryob

Image:Royal Standard of the United Kingdom in Scotland.svg *Source*: http://bibliocm.bibliolabs.com/mwAnon/index.php?title=File:Royal_Standard_of_the_United_Kingdom_in_Scotland.svg *License*: GNU Free Documentation License *Contributors*: User:Barryob

Image:Personal flag of Queen Elizabeth II.svg *Source*: http://bibliocm.bibliolabs.com/mwAnon/index.php?title=File:Personal_flag_of_Queen_Elizabeth_II.svg *License*: GNU Free Documentation License *Contributors*: Denelson83, Fry1989, Homo lupus, Jameslwoodward, Shizhao, TreasuryTag, 1 anonymous edits

File:William Orpen - The Signing of Peace in the Hall of Mirrors, Versailles.jpg *Source*: http://bibliocm.bibliolabs.com/mwAnon/index.php?title=File:William_Orpen_-_The_Signing_of_Peace_in_the_Hall_of_Mirrors,_Versailles.jpg *License*: unknown *Contributors*: Bohème, Burts, Elighthart, IxK85, Kilom691, Martin H., Mattes, Millevache, Mu, Rlbberlin, Skeezix1000, Sofinette, Ssolbergj, Túrelio, Zolo, 7 anonymous edits

Image:ImperialConference.jpg *Source*: http://bibliocm.bibliolabs.com/mwAnon/index.php?title=File:ImperialConference.jpg *License*: Public Domain *Contributors*: Library and Archives Canada / C-000964

File:CommonwealthPrimeMinisters1944.jpg *Source*: http://bibliocm.bibliolabs.com/mwAnon/index.php?title=File:CommonwealthPrimeMinisters1944.jpg *License*: unknown *Contributors*: Library and Archives Canada / C-068672

File:Flag of Ceylon.svg *Source*: http://bibliocm.bibliolabs.com/mwAnon/index.php?title=File:Flag_of_Ceylon.svg *License*: Public Domain *Contributors*: User:Thommy9

File:Flag of Fiji.svg *Source*: http://bibliocm.bibliolabs.com/mwAnon/index.php?title=File:Flag_of_Fiji.svg *License*: Public Domain *Contributors*: Anime Addict AA, Avala, ButterStick, Denelson83, Fry1989, Greentubing, Herbythyme, Homo lupus, Klemen Kocjancic, Krun, Lokal Profil, Mattes, Multichill, Neq00, Nightstallion, Sam916, Urhixidur, Vzb83, 7 anonymous edits

File:Flag of The Gambia.svg *Source*: http://bibliocm.bibliolabs.com/mwAnon/index.php?title=File:Flag_of_The_Gambia.svg *License*: Public Domain *Contributors*: Atamari, Avala, Denniss, Fry1989, Klemen Kocjancic, Mattes, Neq00, Nightstallion, Porao, ThomasPusch, Vzb83, WikipediaMaster, Zscout370, 3 anonymous edits

File:Flag of Ghana.svg *Source*: http://bibliocm.bibliolabs.com/mwAnon/index.php?title=File:Flag_of_Ghana.svg *License*: Public Domain *Contributors*: Benchill, Fry1989, Henswick, Homo lupus, Indolences, Jarekt, Klemen Kocjancic, Neq00, SKopp, ThomasPusch, Threecharlie, Torstein, Zscout370, 4 anonymous edits

File:Flag of Guyana.svg *Source*: http://bibliocm.bibliolabs.com/mwAnon/index.php?title=File:Flag_of_Guyana.svg *License*: Public Domain *Contributors*: User:SKopp

File:Flag of India.svg *Source*: http://bibliocm.bibliolabs.com/mwAnon/index.php?title=File:Flag_of_India.svg *License*: Public Domain *Contributors*: User:SKopp

File:Flag of Ireland.svg *Source*: http://bibliocm.bibliolabs.com/mwAnon/index.php?title=File:Flag_of_Ireland.svg *License*: Public Domain *Contributors*: User:SKopp

File:Flag of Kenya.svg *Source*: http://bibliocm.bibliolabs.com/mwAnon/index.php?title=File:Flag_of_Kenya.svg *License*: Public Domain *Contributors*: User:Pumbaa80

File:Flag of Malawi 1964-2010.svg *Source*: http://bibliocm.bibliolabs.com/mwAnon/index.php?title=File:Flag_of_Malawi_1964-2010.svg *License*: Public Domain *Contributors*: User:SKopp

File:Flag of Malta.svg *Source*: http://bibliocm.bibliolabs.com/mwAnon/index.php?title=File:Flag_of_Malta.svg *License*: unknown *Contributors*: Fry1989, Gabbe, Homo lupus, Klemen Kocjancic, Liftarn, Mattes, Nightstallion, Peeperman, Pumbaa80, Ratatosk, Zscout370, 4 anonymous edits

Image:Royal Standard of Malta (1964).svg *Source*: http://bibliocm.bibliolabs.com/mwAnon/index.php?title=File:Royal_Standard_of_Malta_(1964).svg *License*: Public Domain *Contributors*: Fry1989, Homo lupus, Pumbaa80, Yaddah, 5 anonymous edits

File:Flag of Mauritius.svg *Source*: http://bibliocm.bibliolabs.com/mwAnon/index.php?title=File:Flag_of_Mauritius.svg *License*: Public Domain *Contributors*: User:Gabbe, User:SKopp

Image:Royal Standard of Mauritius.svg *Source*: http://bibliocm.bibliolabs.com/mwAnon/index.php?title=File:Royal_Standard_of_Mauritius.svg *License*: GNU Free Documentation License *Contributors*: User:Barryob

File:Flag of Nigeria.svg *Source*: http://bibliocm.bibliolabs.com/mwAnon/index.php?title=File:Flag_of_Nigeria.svg *License*: Public Domain *Contributors*: User:Jhs

File:Flag of Pakistan.svg *Source*: http://bibliocm.bibliolabs.com/mwAnon/index.php?title=File:Flag_of_Pakistan.svg *License*: Public Domain *Contributors*: Abaezriv, AnonMoos, Badseed, Dbenbenn, Duduziq, F. F. Fjodor, Fry1989, Gabbe, Himasaram, Homo lupus, Juiced lemon, Klemen Kocjancic, Mattes, Mollajutt, Neq00, Pumbaa80, Rfc1394, Srtxg, TFCforever, ThomasPusch, Túrelio, Zscout370, 9 anonymous edits

File:Flag of Sierra Leone.svg *Source*: http://bibliocm.bibliolabs.com/mwAnon/index.php?title=File:Flag_of_Sierra_Leone.svg *License*: Public Domain *Contributors*: Anime Addict AA, Fry1989, Klemen Kocjancic, Kookaburra, Mattes, Nightstallion, Rocket000, ThomasPusch, Zscout370, 1 anonymous edits

File:Flag of South Africa 1928-1994.svg *Source*: http://bibliocm.bibliolabs.com/mwAnon/index.php?title=File:Flag_of_South_Africa_1928-1994.svg *License*: Public Domain *Contributors*: User:Denelson83, User:Denelson83

File:Flag of Tanganyika.svg *Source*: http://bibliocm.bibliolabs.com/mwAnon/index.php?title=File:Flag_of_Tanganyika.svg *License*: GNU Free Documentation License *Contributors*: w:User:MysidMysid

File:Flag of Trinidad and Tobago.svg *Source*: http://bibliocm.bibliolabs.com/mwAnon/index.php?title=File:Flag_of_Trinidad_and_Tobago.svg *License*: Public Domain *Contributors*: AnonMoos, Boricuaeddie, Duduziq, Enbéká, Fry1989, Homo lupus, Klemen Kocjancic, Madden, Mattes, Nagy, Neq00, Nightstallion, Pumbaa80, SKopp, Tomia, 10 anonymous edits

Image:Royal Standard of Trinidad and Tobago.png *Source*: http://bibliocm.bibliolabs.com/mwAnon/index.php?title=File:Royal_Standard_of_Trinidad_and_Tobago.png *License*: Public Domain *Contributors*: Fry1989, Nightstallion, Stannered, 5 anonymous edits

File:Flag of Uganda.svg *Source*: http://bibliocm.bibliolabs.com/mwAnon/index.php?title=File:Flag_of_Uganda.svg *License*: Public Domain *Contributors*: User:Nightstallion

File:Gj-map.gif *Source*: http://bibliocm.bibliolabs.com/mwAnon/index.php?title=File:Gj-map.gif *License*: Public Domain *Contributors*: Arb, Kintetsubuffalo, PoM, Ras67, Telim tor

Image:StGeorgesGrenada2000.jpg *Source*: http://bibliocm.bibliolabs.com/mwAnon/index.php?title=File:StGeorgesGrenada2000.jpg *License*: GNU Free Documentation License *Contributors*: Foroa, Infrogmation, Scanlan, Yrithinnd

File:Grenada-Saint George.png *Source*: http://bibliocm.bibliolabs.com/mwAnon/index.php?title=File:Grenada-Saint_George.png *License*: Creative Commons Attribution-Sharealike 2.5 *Contributors*: User:Golbez

Image:Grenada parishes named.png *Source*: http://bibliocm.bibliolabs.com/mwAnon/index.php?title=File:Grenada_parishes_named.png *License*: Attribution *Contributors*: User:Golbez

File:Grenada-Saint Andrew.png *Source*: http://bibliocm.bibliolabs.com/mwAnon/index.php?title=File:Grenada-Saint_Andrew.png *License*: Creative Commons Attribution-Sharealike 2.5 *Contributors*: User:Golbez

File:Grenada-Saint John.png *Source*: http://bibliocm.bibliolabs.com/mwAnon/index.php?title=File:Grenada-Saint_John.png *License*: Creative Commons Attribution-Sharealike 2.5 *Contributors*: User:Golbez

File:Grenada-Saint Patrick.png *Source*: http://bibliocm.bibliolabs.com/mwAnon/index.php?title=File:Grenada-Saint_Patrick.png *License*: Creative Commons Attribution-Sharealike 2.5 *Contributors*: User:Golbez

File:Grenada location map.svg *Source*: http://bibliocm.bibliolabs.com/mwAnon/index.php?title=File:Grenada_location_map.svg *License*: unknown *Contributors*: NordNordWest, 1 anonymous edits

File:Red pog.svg *Source*: http://bibliocm.bibliolabs.com/mwAnon/index.php?title=File:Red_pog.svg *License*: Public Domain *Contributors*: User:Andux

File:Mt Craven Mt Rodney.jpg *Source*: http://bibliocm.bibliolabs.com/mwAnon/index.php?title=File:Mt_Craven_Mt_Rodney.jpg *License*: Creative Commons Attribution-Sharealike 3.0 *Contributors*: User:Kylekieran

File:Hillsborough Carriacou.jpg *Source*: http://bibliocm.bibliolabs.com/mwAnon/index.php?title=File:Hillsborough_Carriacou.jpg *License*: GNU Free Documentation License *Contributors*: Man, Telim tor

File:hillsborough carriacou.jpg *Source*: http://bibliocm.bibliolabs.com/mwAnon/index.php?title=File:Hillsborough_carriacou.jpg *License*: Public Domain *Contributors*: Original uploader was Jackregan at en.wikipedia

File:CCOU2.JPG *Source*: http://bibliocm.bibliolabs.com/mwAnon/index.php?title=File:CCOU2.JPG *License*: Public Domain *Contributors*: Ratzer, Telim tor

File:carr7885.png *Source*: http://bibliocm.bibliolabs.com/mwAnon/index.php?title=File:Carr7885.png *License*: Public Domain *Contributors*: Original uploader was Caltrop at en.wikipedia

File:carr7109.png *Source*: http://bibliocm.bibliolabs.com/mwAnon/index.php?title=File:Carr7109.png *License*: Public Domain *Contributors*: Original uploader was Caltrop at en.wikipedia

File:Grenada-Saint Mark.png *Source*: http://bibliocm.bibliolabs.com/mwAnon/index.php?title=File:Grenada-Saint_Mark.png *License*: Creative Commons Attribution-Sharealike 2.5 *Contributors*: User:Golbez

File:Fire.svg *Source*: http://bibliocm.bibliolabs.com/mwAnon/index.php?title=File:Fire.svg *License*: Public Domain *Contributors*: User:Indolences

File:Map grenada volcanoes.png *Source*: http://bibliocm.bibliolabs.com/mwAnon/index.php?title=File:Map_grenada_volcanoes.png *License*: Public Domain *Contributors*: Lyn Topinka

Image:Kick-'em-JennySONAR.jpg *Source*: http://bibliocm.bibliolabs.com/mwAnon/index.php?title=File:Kick-'em-JennySONAR.jpg *License*: Public Domain *Contributors*: Doug Martin, NOAA

File:Grenada-Saint David.png *Source*: http://bibliocm.bibliolabs.com/mwAnon/index.php?title=File:Grenada-Saint_David.png *License*: Creative Commons Attribution-Sharealike 2.5 *Contributors*: User:Golbez

File:Gouyave Sign.jpg *Source*: http://bibliocm.bibliolabs.com/mwAnon/index.php?title=File:Gouyave_Sign.jpg *License*: Creative Commons Attribution-Sharealike 3.0 *Contributors*: User:Kylekieran

File:Grenadacricket.jpg *Source*: http://bibliocm.bibliolabs.com/mwAnon/index.php?title=File:Grenadacricket.jpg *License*: Creative Commons Attribution 2.0 *Contributors*: Madmack

File:Airplane silhouette.svg *Source*: http://bibliocm.bibliolabs.com/mwAnon/index.php?title=File:Airplane_silhouette.svg *License*: Public Domain *Contributors*: User:McSush

CPSIA information can be obtained at www.ICGtesting.com
Printed in the USA
LVOW11s0718071113

360342LV00007B/98/P

9 781249 225232